THE ART OF *Soul* COVERS

SCAN THE SPOTIFY CODES TO PLAY EVERY ALBUM INSTANTLY! *

1.
Click the search bar in your **Spotify** app.
Then tip the camera 📷 icon at the top right.

2.
Scan the printed **Spotify** code on the calendar page.

3.
Enjoy the music!

* Please note: Not all bands present themselves on Spotify, so there are various albums without a code.

"The whole point of an album is to understand the artist and enjoy the music - it's supposed to make you want to go to a concert to see them in the flesh and get the album on vinyl and be a part of everything. That's what I'm about."

Little Simz British Rap and Soul Singer / Simbiatu Abisola Abiola Ajikawo

In the early 1960s, a shift occurred in African-American music when singers like Ray Charles and Sam Cooke infused secular lyrics into gospel, departing from the traditional confines of the church. This marked the era of the 7" single, a medium that resonated with a new audience. Early soul LPs mainly comprised compilations of successful singles, enriched with cover versions. However, the landscape underwent a radical transformation in 1971 when Marvin Gaye's 'What's Going On' challenged resistance from his label, Motown. This watershed moment opened the floodgates. Sly & The Family Stone, Stevie Wonder, Isaac Hayes, The Temptations and James Brown – along with numerous overlooked groups – embraced the format as a canvas for social commentary and bold experimentation. Songs expanded beyond the radio-friendly three-minute norm, extending to over ten minutes long. Producers like Norman Whitfield in Detroit and Gamble and Huff in Philadelphia crafted ghetto symphonies on the long-playing medium that the emerging African-American middle class could now afford. This contrasted with the 1960s when civil rights battles still raged: LPs were expensive both to produce and for the consumer. Music also acquired a visual aesthetic, providing a face to the musicians, their stories told through liner notes on the back covers. Lovers of Al Green's voice could now hold him, lounging in a white suit on a wicker chair, in their hands as an LP. Today, original LPs command staggering prices in trading circles; record shops and online exchanges are booming. Despite the rise of the CD and streaming platforms like Spotify, the sublime feeling elicited by vinyl remains unmatched. The feel of the record, the crackle as the needle finds its groove, analogue playback, and the enduring allure of DJ culture all defy the logic of technological progress. As the saying goes, 'the dead live longer': a sentiment that certainly applies to the LP. This calendar pays homage to the unique aura that only an original pressing can have for a diehard collector.

Lars Bulnheim
Vienna, October 2023, Soul DJ, Vinyl Collector, Musician & Journalist

Various Artists
Soul Time
Philips, 1968
Holger Mathies (Design)

01 JAN

The Temptations
Solid Rock
Gordy-Motown Record Corporation, 1971
Curtis McNair (Design)
Hendin (Photo)

02 JAN

Original Soundtrack – Quincy Jones
They Call Me Mister Tibbs
United Artists Records, 1970
Frank Gauna (Design)

03 JAN

Nicole Willis and The Soul Investigators
Keep Reachin Up
Timmion Records, 2005
Pabla Steffa/Njoi Colab (Design)
Mikko Ryhänen (Photo)

04 JAN

Original Motion Picture Soundtrack
Black Fist
Happy Fox Records, 1977
James Graca, Ron Carson (Design)

05 JAN

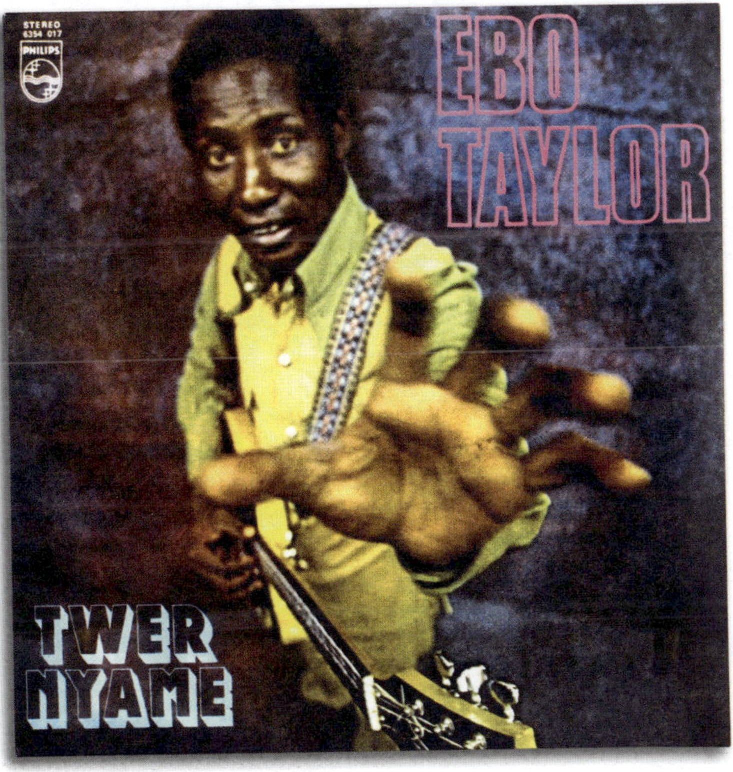

* Jan 6th, 1936
Deroy Taylor
Cape Coast (Ghana)

Ebo Taylor
Twer Nyame
Philips, 1978
Mantsefio Bampoe (Design)
G. Annan-Forson (Photo)

06 JAN

The Supremes
A Bit Of Liverpool
Motown Record Corp., 1964
Yeszin / Mead (Design)

07 JAN

The Brothers
Disco-Soul
People, 1974
Roger Huyssen (Illustration)

08 JAN

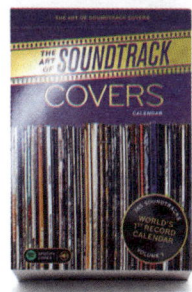

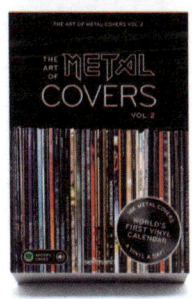

www.seltmannpublishers.com

Worldwide shipping, free within Germany

Durand Jones & The Indications
American Love Call
Dead Oceans, 2019
Miles Johnson & Blake Rhein (Design)
Rosie Cohe (Photo)

09 JAN

Bar-Kays
Too Hot To Stop
Mercury, 1976
Jim Schubert (Design)
Belinda Taylor (Photo)

10 JAN

Kool and The Gang
Good Times
De-Lite Records, 1972
Alfredo Seville (Design)
Alfredo Seville (Illustration)

11 JAN

GEORGE DUKE

"A very special album conceived and recorded in Brazil; a blend of music, musicians and ideas."

A BRAZILIAN LOVE AFFAIR

* Jan 12th, 1946
San Rafael (California)

George Duke
A Brazilian Love Affair
Epic Records, 1980
Vania Toledo (Photo)

12 JAN

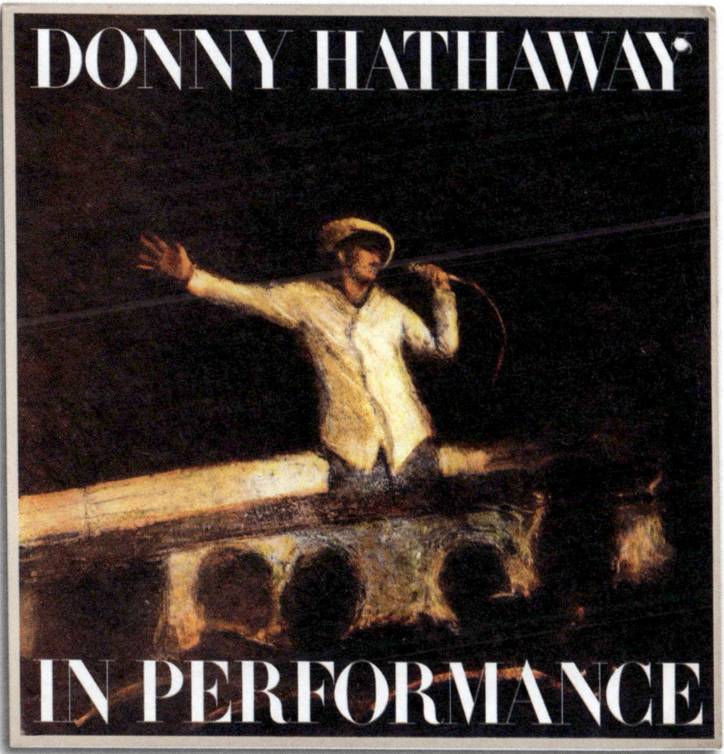

† Jan 13th, 1979
New York City

Donny Hathaway
In Performance
Atlantic Records, 1980
Bob Defrin (Design)
John Collier (Illustration)

13 JAN

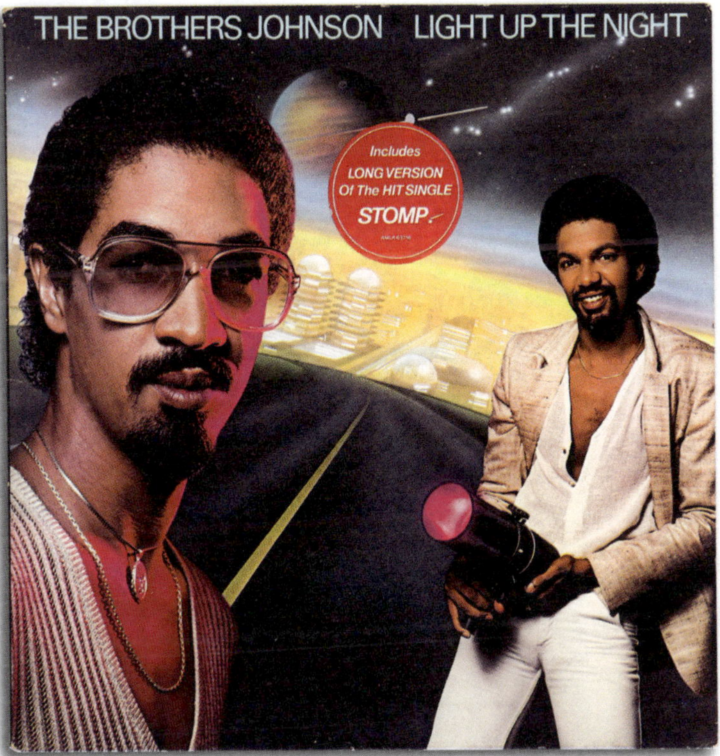

The Brothers Johnson
Light Up The Night
A&M Records, 1980
Chuck Beeson, Glen Wexler (Design)
Glen Wexler (Photo)

14 JAN

Various Artists
The Original Sound Of New Orleans Soul 1966–76
Soul Jazz Records, 2014
Adrian Shelf, Heraldic Charm (Design)

15 JAN

sade *love deluxe*

* Jan 16th, 1959
Helen Folsade Adu
Ibadan (Nigeria)

Sade
Love Deluxe
Epic Records, 1992
Quest Typesetting (Design)
Albert Watson (Photo)

16 JAN

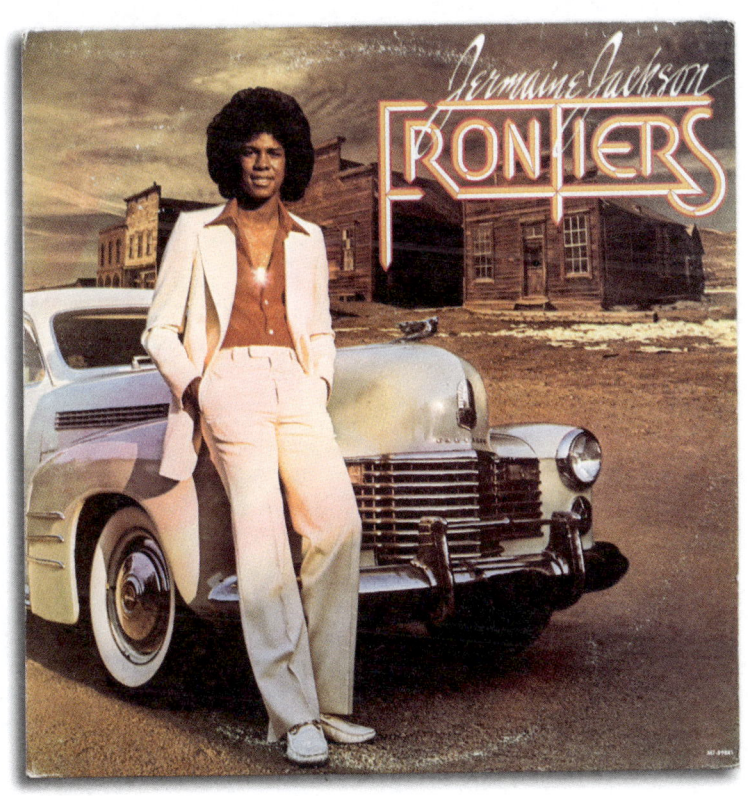

Jermaine Jackson
Frontiers
Motown Records, 1978
Stan Martin (Design)
Sam Emerson (Photo)

17 JAN

Everything's coming up love

David Ruffin

* Jan 18th, 1941
Whynot (Mississippi)

Davis Ruffin
Everything's Coming Up Love
Tamla Motown, 1976
Frank Mulvey (Design)
Norman Seef (Photo)

18 JAN

Wilson Pickett | a funky situation

† Jan 19th, 2006
Reston (Virginia)

Wilson Pickett
A Funky Situation
Big Tree Records, 1978
Lynn Dreese Breslin (Design)
Jim Houghton (Photo)

19 JAN

Gil Scott-Heron
Reflections
Arista, 1981
Donn Davenport (Design)
Vincent Frye (Photo)

20 JAN

* Jan 21st, 1942
Edwin Starr
Nashville (Tennessee)

Edwin Starr & Blinky
Just We Two
Gordy, 1976
Curtis McNair (Design)
Jerry Dempnock (Photo)

21 JAN

Love Unlimited
Under The Influence Of Love Unlimited
PYE International Records, 1973
Barry White (Design)
George Whiteman (Photo)

22 JAN

Mamas Gun
Cure The Jones
Légère Recordings, 2022
Kerstin Holzwarth (Design)
Jodie May Seymour (Illustration)

23 JAN

Various Artists
Funkrock – Compilated By DJ Spinna & Monty Burns
BBE, 2001
Thomas "Badshoes" Mc Callion (Design)
Michael Joseph (Photo)

24 JAN

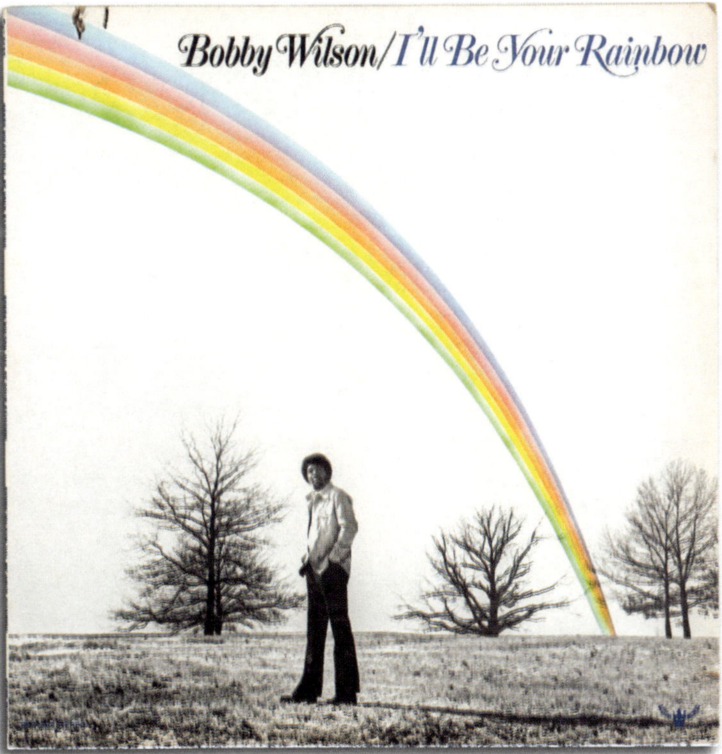

Bobby Wilson
I'll Be Your Rainbow
Buddah Records, 1975
Milton Sincoff (Design)
Hal Wilson (Photo)

25 JAN

Various Artists
Let's Clean Up The Ghetto
Philadelphia International Records, 1977
Ed Lee (Design)
John Pinderhughes (Photo)

26 JAN

* Jan 27th, 1941
Robert "Bobby" Hutcherson
Los Angeles (California)

Bobby Hutcherson
Total Eclipse
Blue Note, 1968
Forlenza Venosa Associates (Design)
Rob van Petten (Photo)

27   JAN

**The 5th Dimension
Greatest Hits On Earth**
Bell Records, 1972
Beverly Weinstein (Design)
Ed Caraeff (Photo)

28 JAN

* Jan 29th, 1994
Brittney Denise Parks
Cincinnati (Ohio)

Sudan Archives
Sink
Stones Throw Records, 2018
Jeff Jank (Design)
Jack McCain (Photo)

29 JAN

Igna Igwebuike
Bomp
PMG, 2016
Jinbrin Sons Photos (Photo)

30 JAN

Grand Funk
Grand Funk Hits
Capitol Records, 1976
Keith Sheridan, Migel Sanchez, Peter Corriston (Design)
Lynn Goldsmith (Photo)

31 JAN

† Feb 1st, 2013
Cecil Womack
Johannesburg (South Africa)

Womack & Womack
Conscience
Island Records, 1988
Carol Friedman (Design)

01 FEB

* Feb 2nd, 1979
Andrew Mayer Cohen
Ann Arbor (Michigan)

Mayer Hawthorne
A Strange Arrangement
Stones Throw Records, 2009
Jeff Jank (Design)
Jeremy Deputant (Photo)

02 FEB

* Feb 3rd, 1935
Houston (Texas)

Johnny Guitar Watson
Giant
DJM Records, 1978
DFK / David Krieger (Design)
Jim McCrary (Photo)

03 FEB

New Birth
Love Potion
Warner Bros. Records, 1976
Bob Lockart (Design)
Norman Seeff (Photo)

04 FEB

* Feb 5th, 1950
Mary Burton
Greenville (South Carolina)

Ann Sexton
The Beginning
Sound Stage 7, 1977
Ken Kim (Design)

05 FEB

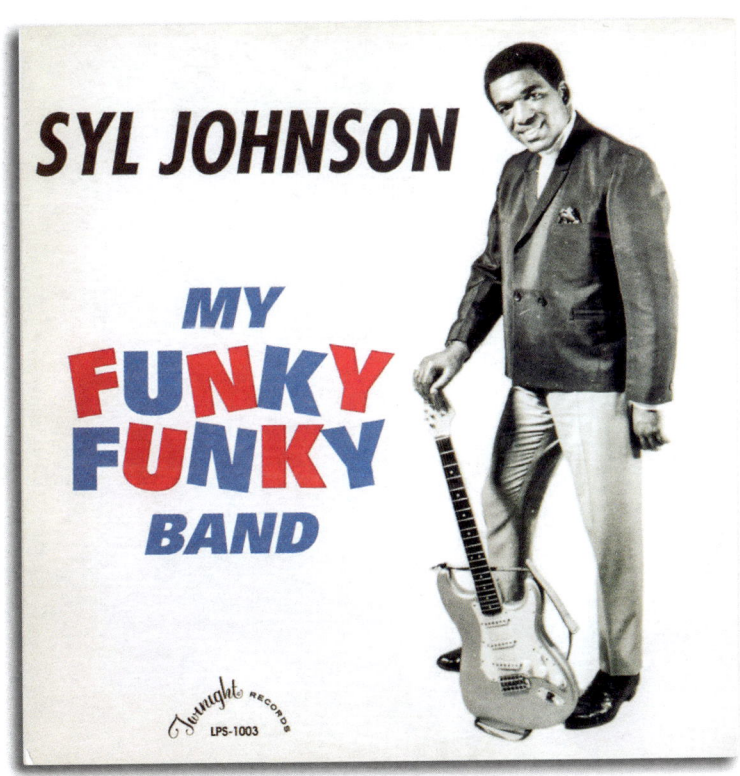

† Feb 6th, 2022
Sylvester Thompson
Mableton (Georgia)

Syl Johnson
My Funky Funky Band
Numero Group, 2017
Cover Artists Unknown

06 FEB

* Feb 7th, 1934
Curtis Ousley
Fort Worth (Texas)

King Curtis
Instant Groove
ATCO Records, 1969
Haig Adishian (Design)
Steven Paley (Photo)

07 FEB

The Jacksons
Epic, 1976
John Berg (Design)
Harou Miyauchi (Photo)

08 FEB

† Feb 9th, 2022
Betty Gray Mabry
Homestead (Pennsylvania)

Betty Davis
Just Sunshine Records, 1973
Ron Levine (Design)
Mel Dixon (Photo)

09 FEB

* Feb 10th, 1937
Black Mountain (North Carolina)

Roberta Flack
Killing Me Softly
Atlantic Records, 1973
Rod Dyer, Inc. (Design)
Burt Goldblatt (Photo)

10 FEB

* Feb 11th, 1942
Otha Leon Haywood
Houston (Texas)

Leon Haywood
Naturally
20th Century Fox Records, 1980
Stan Martin (Design)
Jim Britt (Photo)

11 FEB

Various Artists
That's Soul 6
Atlantic Records, 1977
Cover Artists Unknown

12 FEB

Eji Oyewole
Me & You
Presch Media Gmbh, 1975
Floyd Patterson (Design)

13 FEB

The Temptations
Puzzle People
Gordy, 1969
Curtis McNair (Design)
P. Bass (Photo)

14 FEB

The Dells
The Mighty Mighty Dells
Cadet, 1974
David Fried Krieger, Ted Amber (Design)
Axel Ebel (Illustration)

15 FEB

LEON WARE *ROCKIN' YOU ETERNALLY*

* Feb 16th, 1940
Detroit (Michigan)

Leon Ware
Rockin' You Eternally
Elektra/Be With Records, 1981
Norm Ung, Ron Coro (Design)
Beverly Parker (Photo)

16 FEB

The Miracles
Don't Cha Love It
Motown Record Corp., 1975
Katarina Petterson (Design)
Bob Gleason (Illustration)

17 FEB

*Feb 18th, 1952
Veronica Randy Crawford
Macon (Georgia)

Randy Crawford
Everything Must Change
Warner Bros. Records, 1976
Stan Evenson, Vartan Kurjian (Design)
Lisa Powers (Photo)

18 FEB

* Feb 19th, 1940
William Smokey Robinson, Jr.
Detroit (Michigan)

Smokey Robinson
The Tracks Of My Tears
Dino Entertainment, 1980
Damn Fine Design (Design)
Mental Block (Photo)

19 FEB

Instant Funk
Witch Doctor
Salsoul Records, 1979
Stanley Hochstadt (Design)
Len Kaltmann (Photo)

20 FEB

The Meters
Look-Ka Py Py
Josie, 1970
The Graffiteria (Design)
The Graffiteria (Photo)

21 FEB

Various Artists
Soul Sides Volume One
Zealous Records, 2006
David Bias (Design)

22 FEB

† Feb 23rd, 2017
Marina del Rey (California)

Leon Ware
Rainbow Deux
Be With Records, 2019
Ilene Weingard (Design)
Leon Ware (Illustration)

23 FEB

Original Motion Picture Soundtrack
Best Of Car Wash
MCA Records, 1976
Cover Artists Unknown

24 FEB

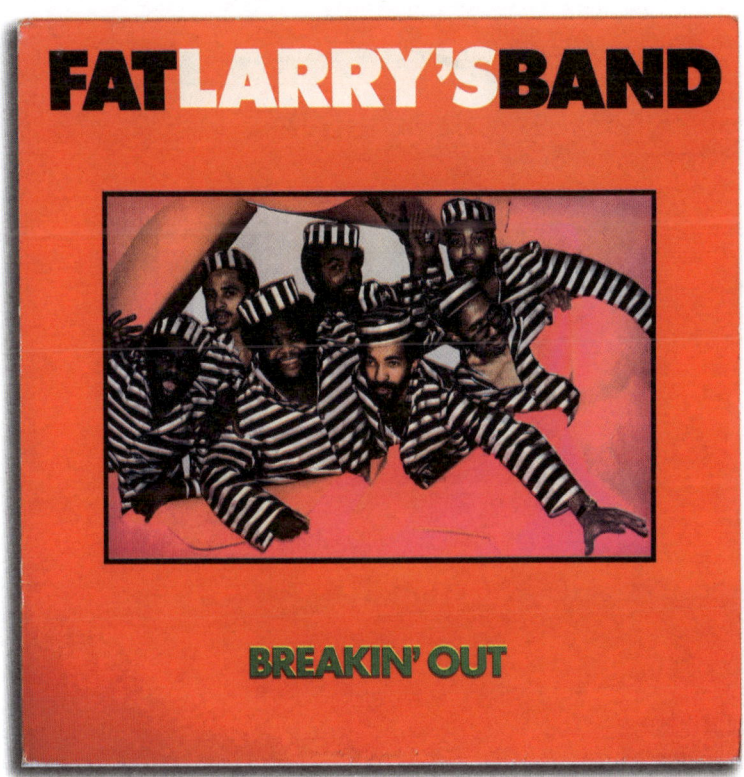

Fat Larry's Band
Breakin Out
WMOT Records, 1982
Roland Young (Design)
Ben Robinson (Photo)

25 FEB

* Feb 26th, 1971
Erica Abi Wright
Dallas (Texas)

Erykah Badu
Mama's Gun
Music on Vinyl / Motown, 2014
Erikah Badu, Mickey Whitfield (Design)
Robert Maxwell (Photo)

26 FEB

The Stylistics
Let's Put It All Together
AVCO, 1974
Maurer Productions, Michael Mendel (Design)
Doug Johnson, Jim O'Connell (Illustration)

27 FEB

Maze feat. Frankie Beverly
Don't Stop The Love
Capitol Records, 1985
Roy Kohara (Design)
Montxo Algora (Illustration)

28 FEB

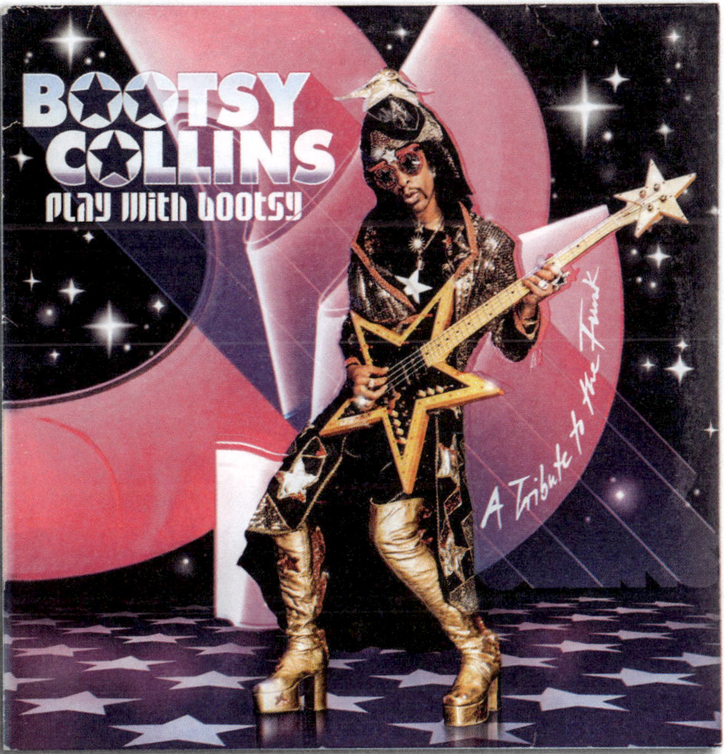

Bootsy Collins
Play With Bootsy – A Tribute To The Funk
Eastwest, 2002
Mick Klaak (Design)
Berry Behrendt (Photo)

29 FEB

The Dells
Greatest Hits
Cadet, 1969
Don Wislon (Illustration)

01 MAR

Various Artists
Groovy Anthems By Kings Of The Funk
Wagram Music, 2021
Supercinq (Design)
Susan Meiselas (Photo)

02 MAR

The Crystals
He's A Rebel
Philles Records, 1963
Yak (Illustration)

03 MAR

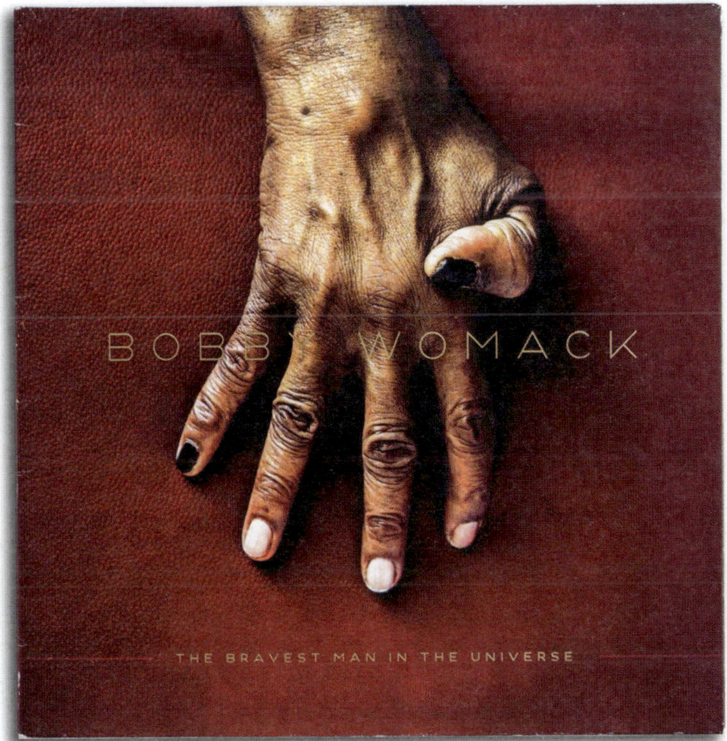

Bobby Womack
The Bravest Man In The Universe
XL Recordings, 2012
Switzerlandcs (Design)
Jamie-James Medina (Photo)

04 MAR

Michael Jackson
Bad
Epic Records, 1987
Tony Lane / Nancy Donald (Design)
Sam Emerson (Photo)

05 MAR

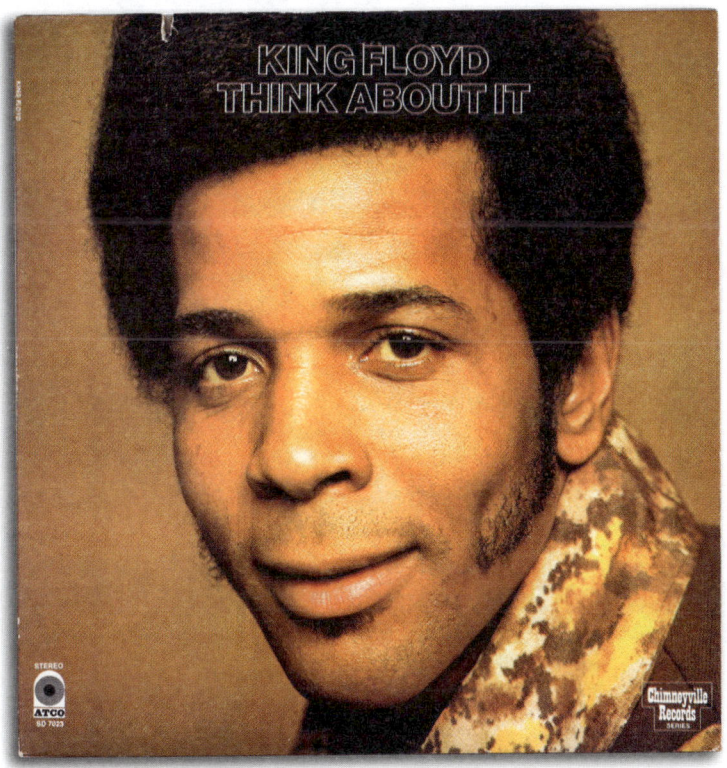

† Mar 6th, 2006
Jackson (California)

King Floyd III
Think About It
ATCO Records, 1973
Haig Adishian (Design)
Joel Brodsky (Photo)

06 MAR

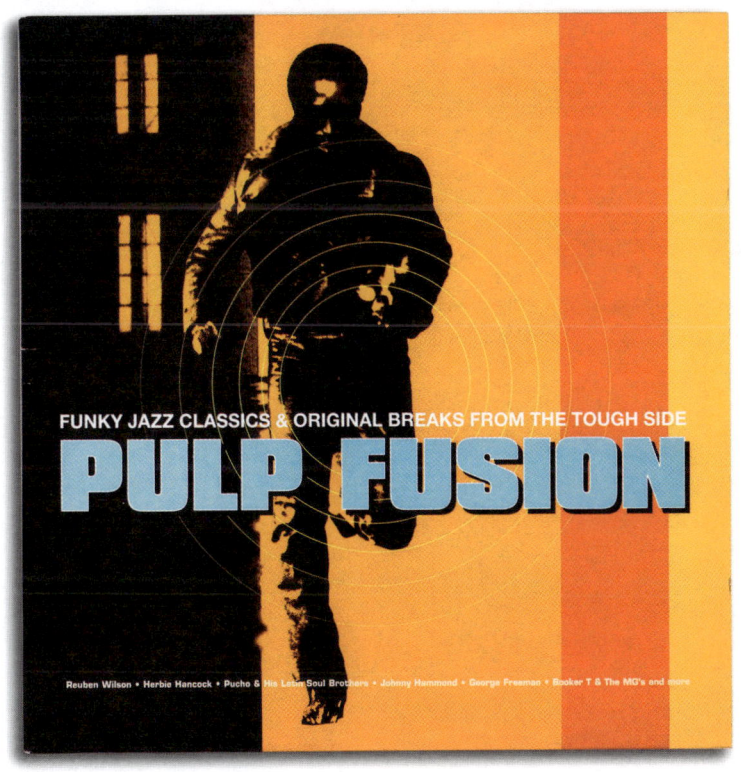

Various Artists
Pulp Fusion
Harmless Recordings, 1997
K 8 Intro, London (Design)
Superfly Video (Photo)

07 MAR

Frankie Smith
Children Of Tomorrow
WMOT Records, 1981
Arnie Roberts (Design)
Jack Swen (Photo)

08 MAR

* Mar 9th, 1945
Laura Lee Newton
Chicago (Illinois)

Laura Lee
Love More Than Pride
Chess, 1972
Maurer Productions (Design)

09   MAR

* Mar 10th, 1964
Neneh Marianne Karlsson
Chicago (Illinois)

Neneh Cherry
Raw Like Sushi
Circa, 1989
Committee (Design)
Jean-Baptiste Mondino (Photo)

10 MAR

The Delfonics
Philly Groove Records, 1970
Bevery Weinstein (Design)
Joel Brodsky (Photo)

11 MAR

*Mar 12th, 1947
Ruby Stackhouse
Hollandale (Mississippi)

Ruby Andrews
Everybody Saw You
Zodiac Records/Everland, 2018
Okamato/London Studio, Inc. (Design)

12 MAR

Attitudes
Good News
Dark Horse Records, 1977
Bob Cato (Design)

13 MAR

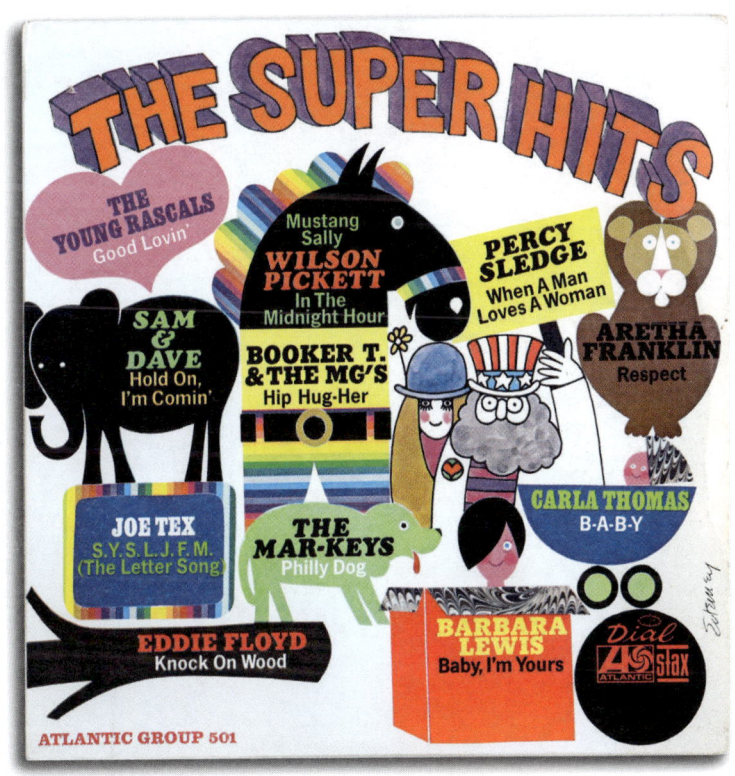

Various Artists
The Super Hits
Atlantic Stax, 1967
Loring Eutemy (Design)

14 MAR

* Mar 15th, 1943
Sylvester Stewart
Dallas (Texas)

Sly & The Family Stone
Fresh
Epic Records, 1973
John Berg (Design)
Richard Avedon (Photo)

15 MAR

Sinkane
Depayse
City Slang, 2019
Aaron Lowell Denton (Design)
Tiffany Smith (Photo)

16 MAR

The Brothers Johnson
Look Out For #1
A&M Records, 1976
Roland Young (Design)
Elliot Gilbert (Photo)

17 MAR

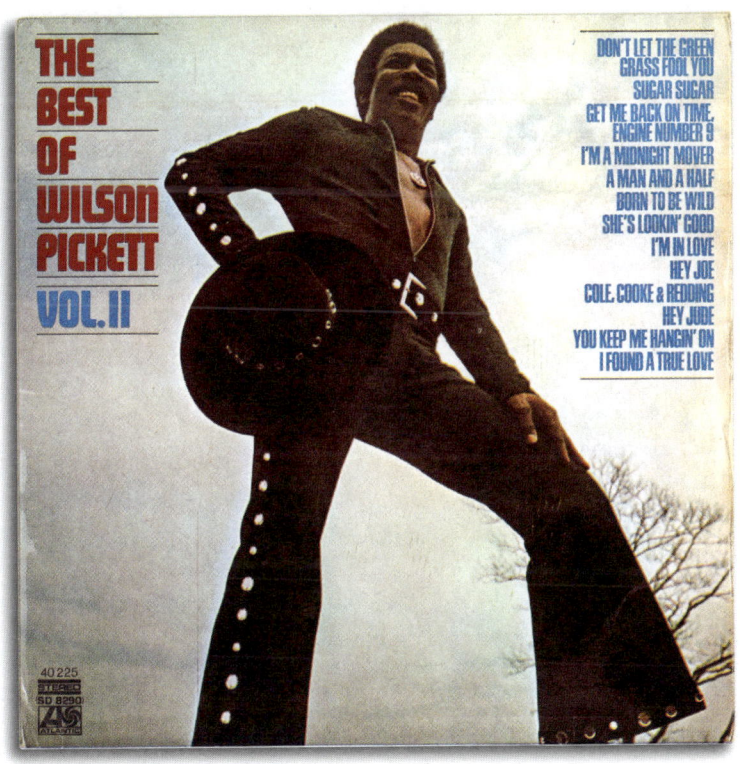

* Mar 18th, 1941
Prattville (Alabama)

Wilson Pickett
The Best Of Wilson Pickett Vol. II
Atlantic Records, 1971
Haig Adishian (Design)
Jim Cummins (Photo)

18 MAR

Soulful Dynamics
Decca, 1971
Cover Artists Unknown

19 MAR

WAR
All Day Music
LAX Records, 1971
Lee Oskar & Howard Miller (Design)
Bob Gordon (Photo)

20 MAR

Gladys Knight & The Pips
Neither One Of Us
Motown Records, 1973
Cover Artists Unknown

21 MAR

* Mar 22nd, 1943
Pittsburgh (Pennsylvania)

George Benson
In Flight
Warner Bros. Records, 1977
Mike Doud (Design)
Antonin Kratochvil (Photo)

22 MAR

The Watts 103rd Street Rhythm Band
Hot Heat And Sweet Groove
Warner Bros. Records, 1968
Ed Trasher (Design)
Bob Zoell (Illustration)

23 MAR

* Mar 24th, 1991
Cleopatra Nikolic
Ladbroke Grove (London)

Cleo Soul
Rose In The Dark
Forever Living Originals, 2020
Cover Artists Unknown

24 MAR

*Mar 25th, 1942
Aretha Louise Franklin
Memphis (Tennessee)

Aretha Franklin
Aretha
Arista, 1986
Andy Warhol (Design)
John Pinderhughes (Photo)

25 MAR

* Mar 26th, 1944
Diana Ernestine Earle Ross
Detroit (Michigan)

Diana Ross
Ross
Motown, 1978
Rickey Ricardo Gaskins (Illustration)

26 MAR

The Meters
Cabbage Alley
Reprise Records, 1972
Ed Trasher (Design)
David Willardson (Photo)

27 MAR

Al Green
I'm Still In Love With You
Hi Records, 1972
Cover Artists Unknown

28 MAR

**Ike Turner Presents The Family Vibes
Confined To Soul**
United Artists Records, 1973
Ron Slenzak (Photo)
Robert Grossman (Illustration)

29 MAR

† Mar 30th, 2020
William Harrison Withers, Jr.
L.A. (California)

Bill Withers
Still Bill
Sussex Records, 1972
Michael Mendel (Design)
Hal Wilson (Photo)

30   MAR

Creative Source
Migration
Sussex Records, 1974
Carl Overr (Design)
Suzanne Ayres (Photo)

31 MAR

† Apr 1st, 1984
Marvin Pentz Gay, Jr.
Washington D.C.

Marvin Gaye
What's Going On
Tamla Motown, 1971
Curtis McNair (Design)
Hendin (Photo)

01 APR

Various Artists
The Very Best Of Motown Love Songs Vol. 1
Telstar, 1984
John Gordon (Design)
Mark Thomas (Illustration)

02 APR

Prince Charles And The City Beat Band
Combat Zone
Virgin, 1984
Da Gama (Design)
John Waricker-Le Breton (Photo)

03 APR

Shalamar
Big Fun
RCA Victor, 1979
Gribbitt!, Henry Vizcarra, Tim Bryant (Design)
Ron Slenzak (Photo)

04 APR

Four Tops
Greatest Hits
Tamla Motown, 1968
Cover Artists Unknown

05 APR

Kellee Patterson
Kellee
Shadybrock Records, 1976
Mort Witz (Photo)

06 APR

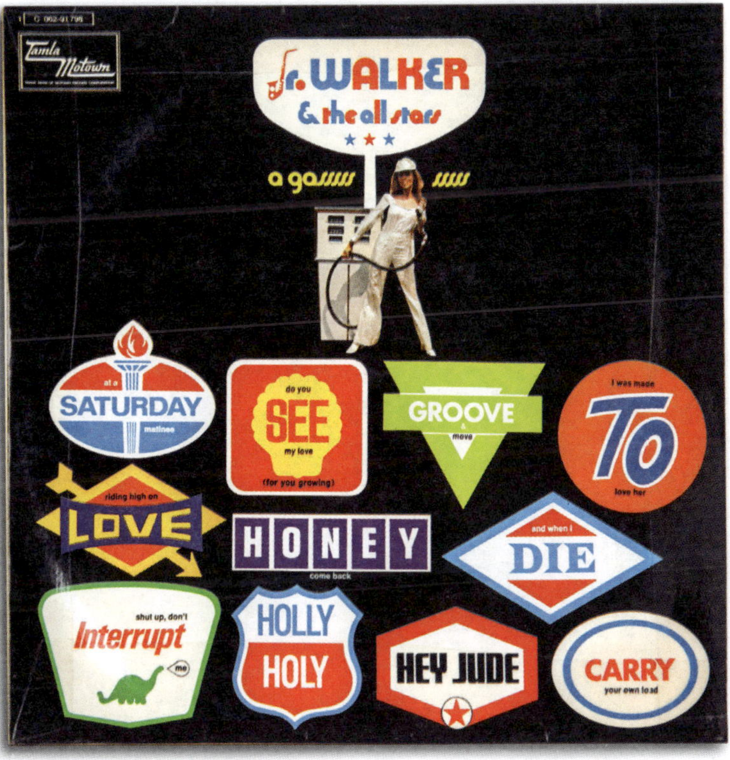

Jr. Walker & The All Stars
A Gasssss
Tamla Motown, 1970
Curtis McNair (Design)
Jim Ladwig, Tom Schlesinger (Photo)

07 APR

Soulful Dynamics
Wildcats
Decca, 1972
Cover Artists Unknown

08 APR

Curtis Mayfield
There's No Place Like America Today
Buddah Records, 1975
Ed Trasher (Design)
Peter Palombi (Illustration)

09 APR

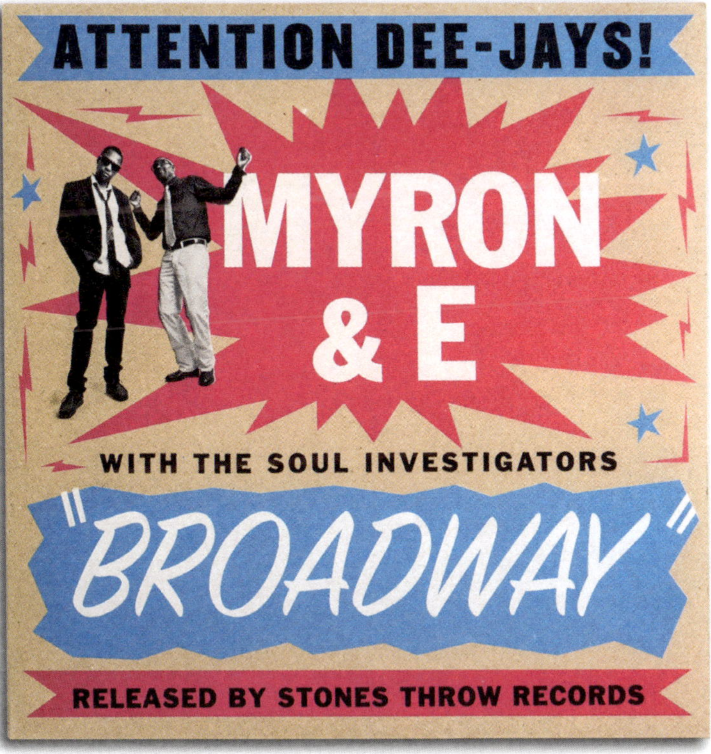

Myron & E with The Soul Investigators
Broadway
Stones Throw Records, 2013
Jeff Jank (Design)
William Perls (Photo)

10 APR

Leon Haywood
Come And Get Yourself Some
20 Century Records, 1975
Queens Graphics (Design)
Buddy Rosenberg & Bob Levy (Photo)

11 APR

The Platters
Sweet, Sweet Lovin'
Musicor Records, 1968
Cover Artists Unknown

12 APR

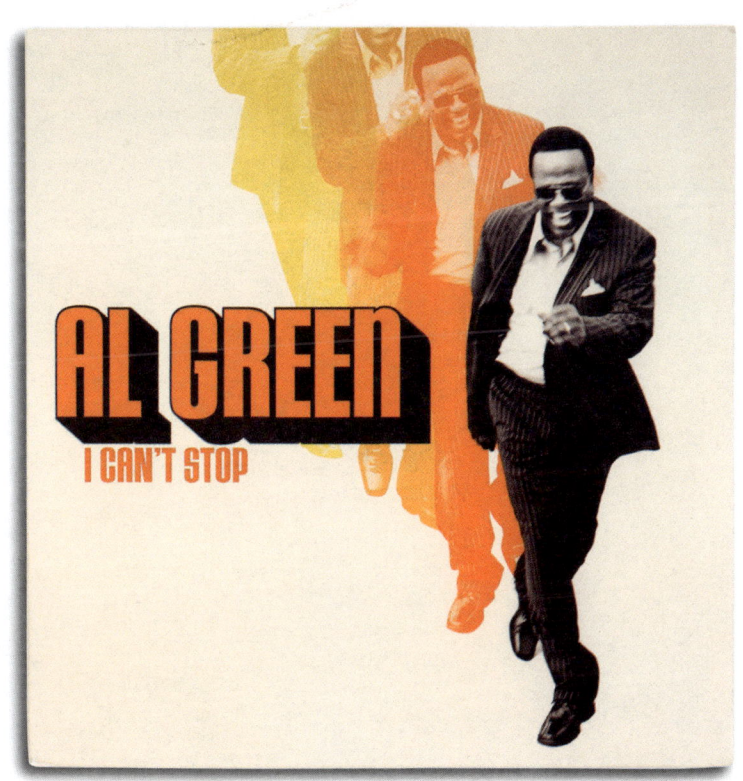

* Apr 13th, 1946
Albert Greene
Forrest City (Arkansas)

Al Green
I Can't Stop
Blue Note, 2003
Burton Yount (Design)
Clay Patrick McBride (Photo)

13 APR

† Apr 14th, 2015
Percy Tyrone Sledge
Baton Rouge (Louisiana)

Percy Sledge
The Best Of
Atlantic Records, 1969
Loring Eutemey (Design)
Joel Brodsky (Photo)

14 APR

The Friends of Distinction
Real Friends
RCA Victor, 1970
Frank Mulwey (Design)
Dave Wilcox (Illustration)

15 APR

Tamiko Jones
Love Trip
Arista, 1975
Nancy Greenberg (Design)
Richard L. Shaefer (Photo)

16 APR

The Fabulous Trammps
The Legendary Zing Album
Buddah Records, 1975
Milton Sincoff (Design)
J. Paul Simone (Photo)

17 APR

Cymande
Janus Records, 1972
Steve Scipio (Design)

18 APR

Rahni Harris & Family Love
A Different Drummer
Emprise, 1977
Murray Brenman (Design)

19 APR

Hot Chocolate
Love Shot
RAK Records, 1983
The Artful Dodgers (Design)

20 APR

† Apr 21st, 2016
Prince Rogers Nelson
Chanhassen (Minnesota)

Prince And The Revolution
Purple Rain
Warner Bros. Records, 1984
Prince (Design)
Ed Trasher (Photo)

21 APR

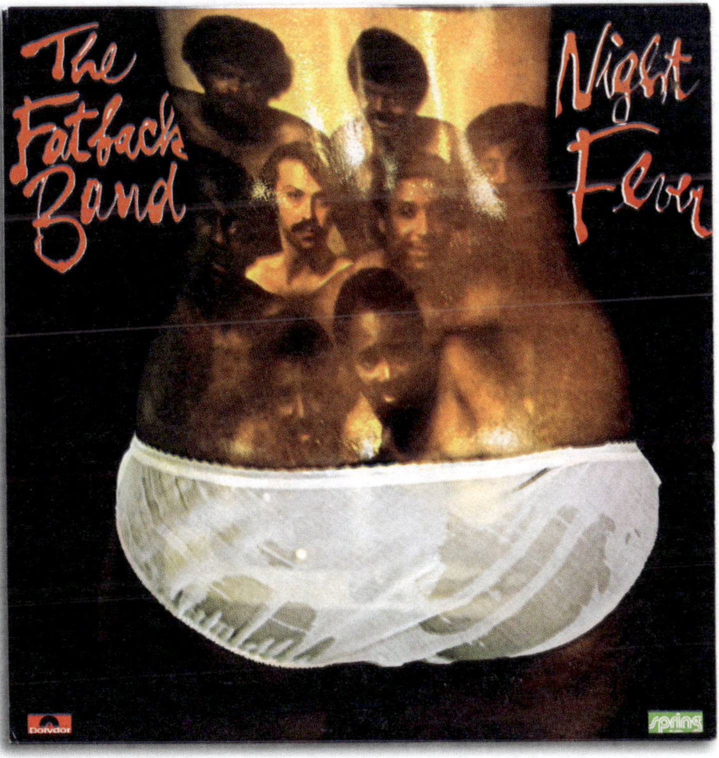

The Fatback Band
Night Fever
Polydor, 1976
Peter Corriston (Design)
Alen MacWeeney (Photo)

22 APR

Lack Of Afro
Hello Baby
Loa Records, 2016
Bunker London (Design)
Emma Gibbons (Illustration)

23 APR

† Apr 24th, 2016
Paul Williams
Blackwood (New Jersey)

Billy Paul
War Of The Gods
Philadelphia International Records, 1973
Ed Lee (Design)
Roger Hane (Illustration)

24 APR

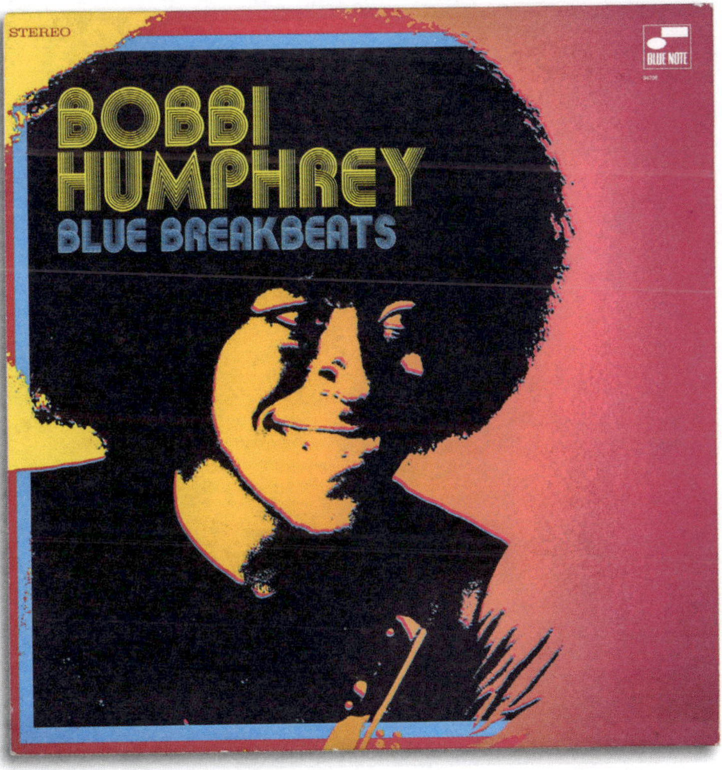

* Apr 25th, 1950
Barbara Ann "Bobbi" Humphrey
Marlin (Texas)

Bobbi Humphrey
Blue Breakbeats
Blue Note, 1998
Patrick Roques (Design)
Michael Ochs Archive (Photo)

25 APR

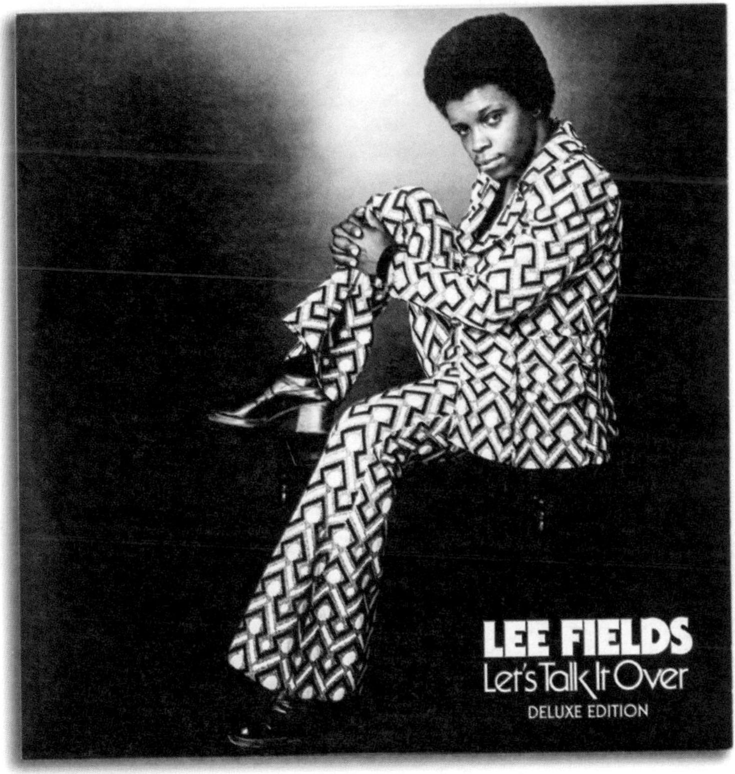

* Apr 26th, 1950
Elmer Lee Fields
Wilson (North Carolina)

Lee Fields
Let's Talk It Over
Truth & Soul, 2012
Truth & Soul (Design)

26 APR

The Stylistics
Fabulous
H & L Records, 1976
Michael Mendel (Design)
Kwane Brathwaite (Photo)

27 APR

Earth, Wind & Fire
The Best Of Earth Wind & Fire Vol. I
CBS Records, 1978
Shusei Nagaoka (Design)

28 APR

Parliament
The Clones Of Dr. Funkenstein
Casablanca, 1976
Chris Whorf, Gribbitt! (Design)

29 APR

Diana Ross & The Supremes with The Temptations
Together
Tamla Motown, 1969
Craig Braun (Design)

30 APR

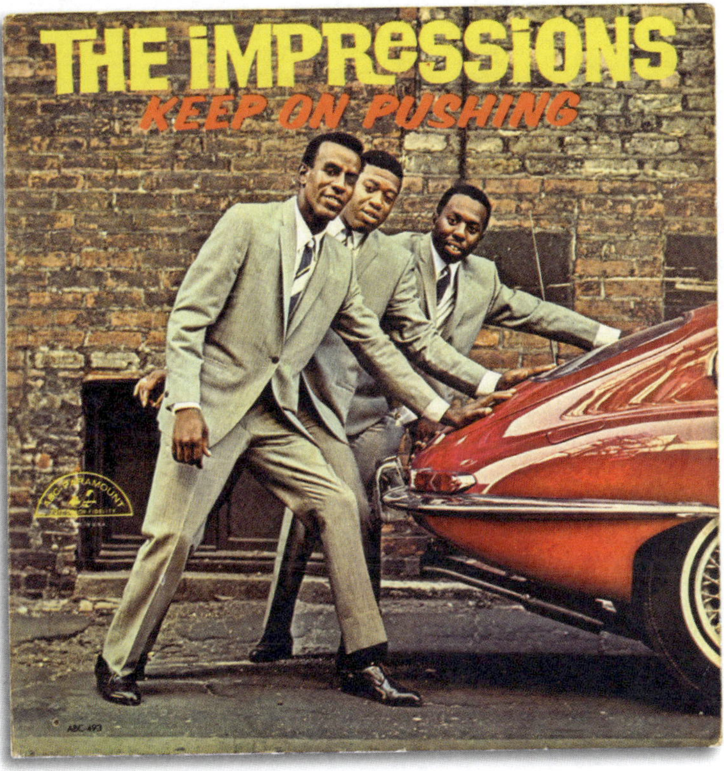

The Impressions
Keep On Pushing
ABC Records, 1965
Joe Lebow (Design)
Don Bronstein (Photo)

01   MAY

Various Artists
Kind Of Soul
Small, 2000
Jean Paul Fernandez (Design)

02 MAY

* May 3rd, 1933
James Joseph Brown, Jr.
Barnwell (South Carolina)

James Brown & The Famous Flames
Live At The Garden
King Records, 1967
Cover Artists Unknown

03 MAY

20 %
PREORDER DISCOUNT!

Get the new vinyl covers calendar with highest discount until June, 30th.

www.seltmannpublishers.com
Worldwide shipping, free within Germany

* May 4th, 1956
Sharon Lafaye Jones
Augusta (Georgia)

Sharon Jones & The Dap-Kings
100 Days 100 Nights
Daptone Records, 2007
David Serre & Anne Coombs (Design)
Dulce Pinzón (Photo)

04 MAY

**The Supremes
A' Go-Go**
Motown, 1966
Horace Junior (Design)
Frank Dandridge (Photo)

05 MAY

The Chanter Sisters
First Flight
Polydor, 1976
Ian Murray (Design)
Moore-Morris (Illustration)

06 MAY

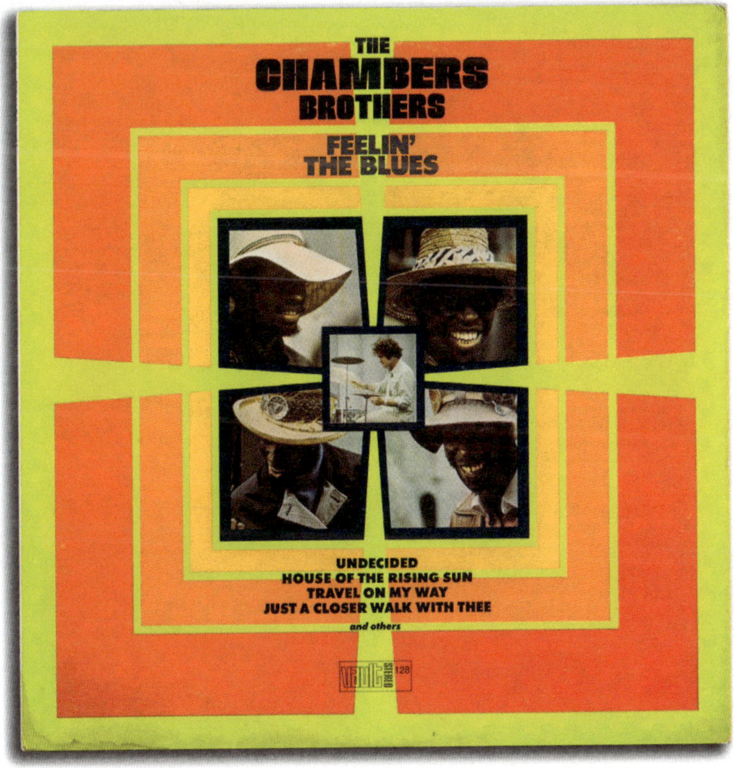

The Chambers Brothers
Feelin' The Blues
Vault, 1970
Gabor Halmos (Design)
Craig Simpson (Photo)

07 MAY

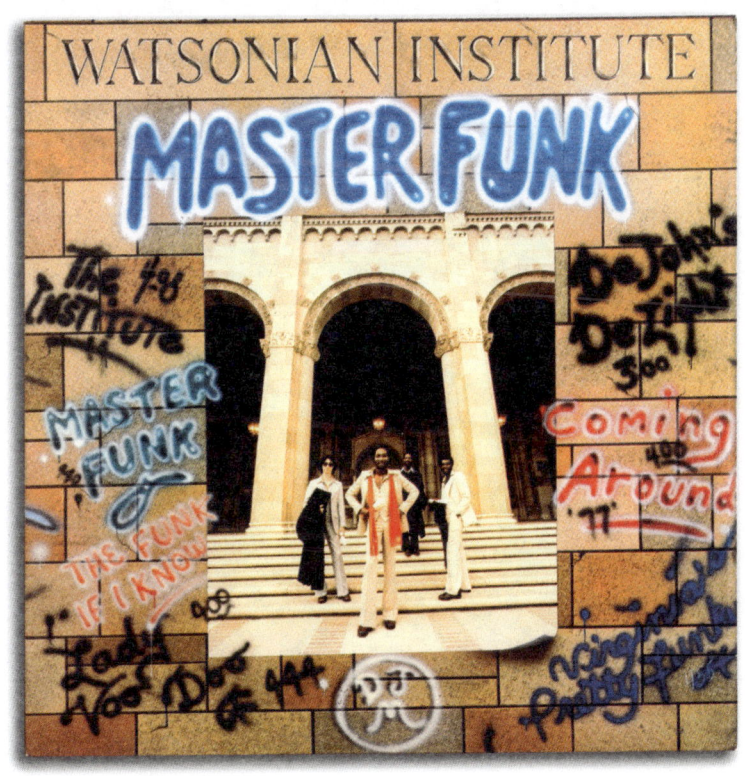

Master Funk
Watsonian Institute
DJM Records, 1978
Don Brautigan (Design)
Tim McCrary (Photo)

08 MAY

Original Motion Soundtrack – James Brown
Slaughter's Big Rip-Off
Polydor, 1973
Charles Bobbitt (Design)

09 MAY

John KaSandra
Color Me Human
Respect, 1970
David Krieger, The Graffiteria (Design)
Joel Brodsky (Photo)

10 MAY

Kool & The Gang
Emergency
De-Lite Records, 1984
Joni Weinstein (Design)
Brian Hagiwara (Photo)

11 MAY

Cane and Able
Epic / AKT, 1972
Henri Tullio (Photo)

12 MAY

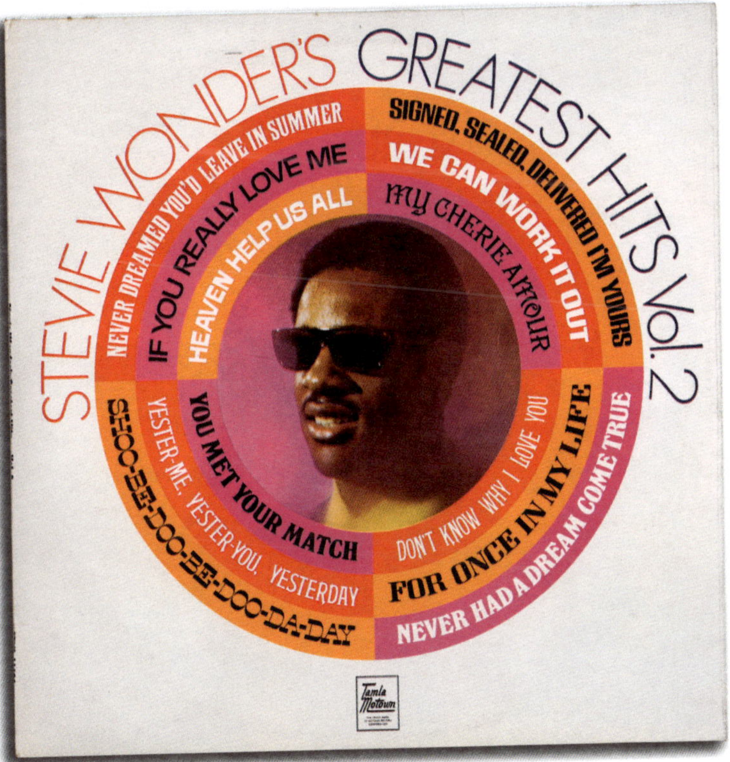

* May 13th, 1950
Stevland Hardaway Judkins Morris
Saginaw (Michigan)

Stevie Wonder
Greatest Hits Vol. 2
Tamla Motown, 1971
Curtis McNair (Design)

13 MAY

Various Artists Numero 066
Afterschool Special: The 123s Of Kid Soul
Numero Group, 2016
Jaffa at The Unknown (Design)

14 MAY

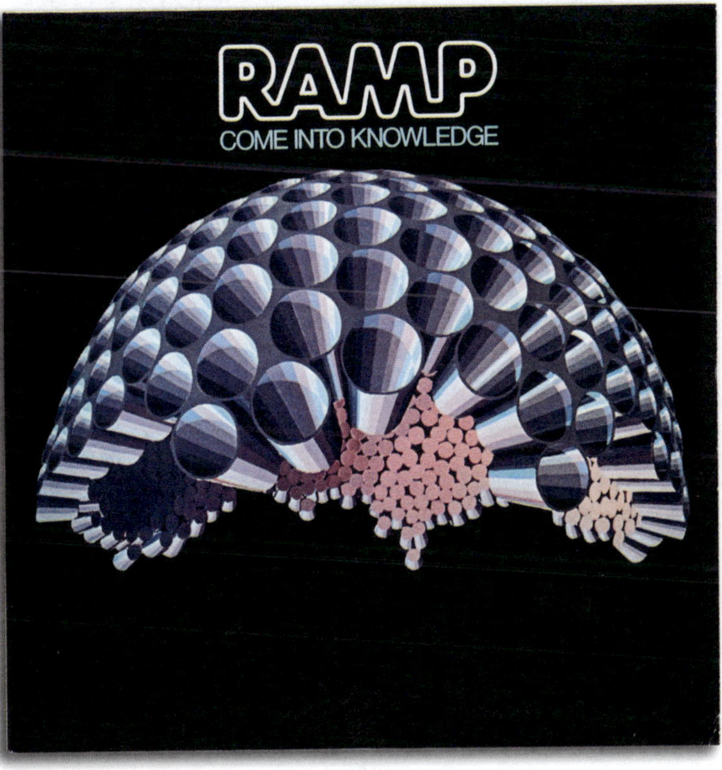

Ramp
Come Into Knowledge
ABC Blue Thumb, 1977
Kats Abe (Design)
Masaki Sato (Illustration)

15 MAY

RUPA
Disco Jazz
Megaphone / Numero Group, 1982
Cover Artists Unknown

16 MAY

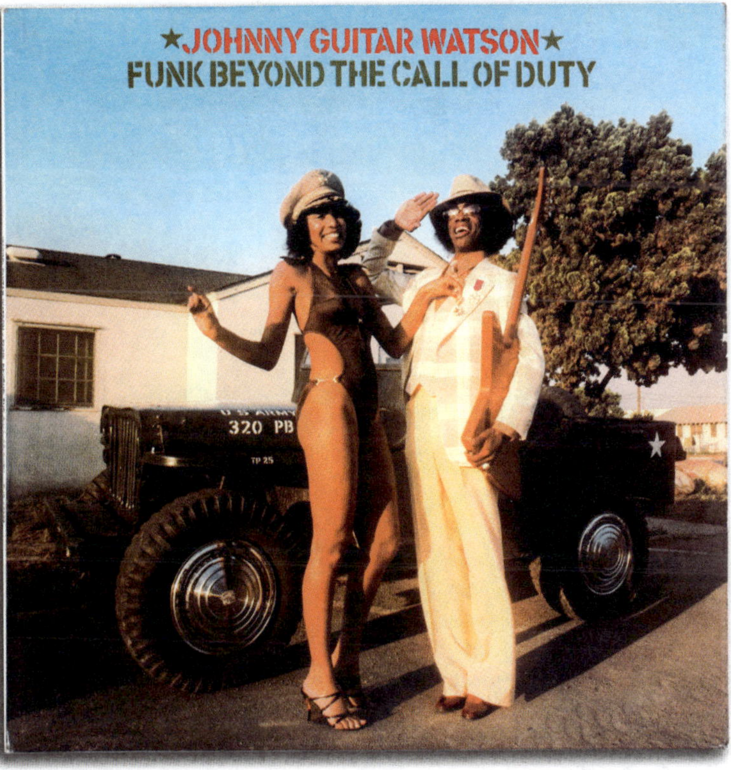

† May 17th, 1996
Yokohama (Japan)

Johnny Guitar Watson
Funk Beyond The Call Of Duty
DJM Records, 1977
David Krieger (Design)
Jim McCrary (Photo)

17 MAY

* May 18th, 1934
Philadelphia (Pennsylvania)

Jack Ashford
Hotel Sheet
Magic Disc Records, Everland, 1977
Alvin R. Hogan (Design)

18 MAY

* May 19th, 1948
Spanish Town Kingston (Jamaica)

Grace Jones
Fame
Island Records, 1978
Neil Terk (Design)
Richard Bernstein (Illustration)

19   MAY

* May 20th, 1946
Cherilyn Sarkisian
El Centro (California)

Sonny & Cher
ATCO Records, 1967
Günter Zint (Photo)

20 MAY

* May 21st, 1953
Detroit Michigan (Michigan)

Carl Carlton
Everlasting Love
ABC Records, 1974
Stan Martin (Design)
Stan Martin (Illustration)

21 MAY

Four Tops
Keeper Of The Castle
Probe/Hörzu, 1972
Ruby Mazur (Design)

22   MAY

Curtis Mayfield
Roots
Buddah Records, 1971
Gil Ross (Photo)

23 MAY

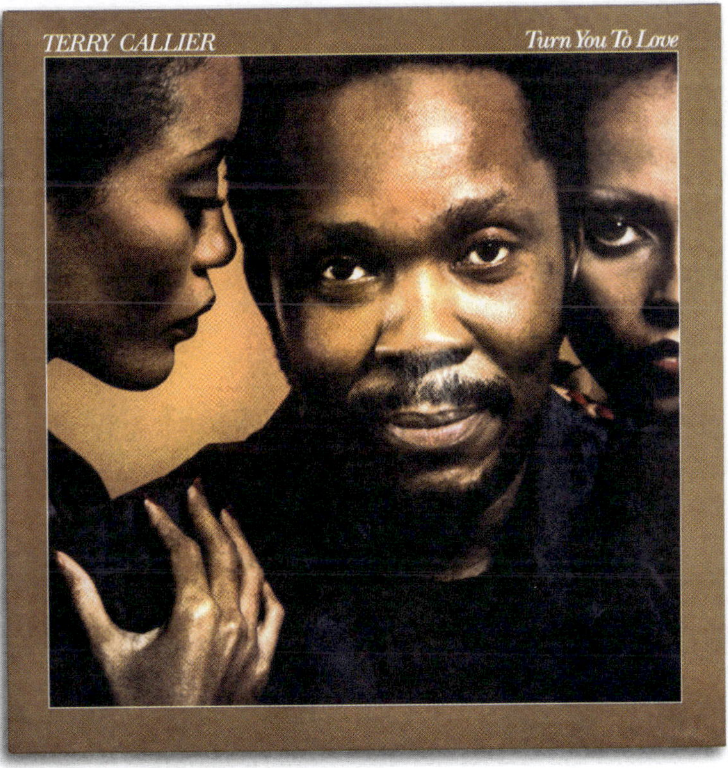

* May 24th, 1945
Chicago Illinois (Illinois)

Terry Callier
Turn You To Love
Elektra, 1979
Ron Coro (Design)

24 MAY

† May 25th, 2013
Tyrone Brunson
Washington D.C. (USA)

Tyrone Brunson
Fresh
Epic, 1984
John Berg (Design)
Mark Raboy (Photo)

25 MAY

Various Artists
Doing Our Thing – More Soul From Jamdown 1970–82
Cree Records, 2017
Merten Kaatz (Design)
Dave Hendley (Photo)

26 MAY

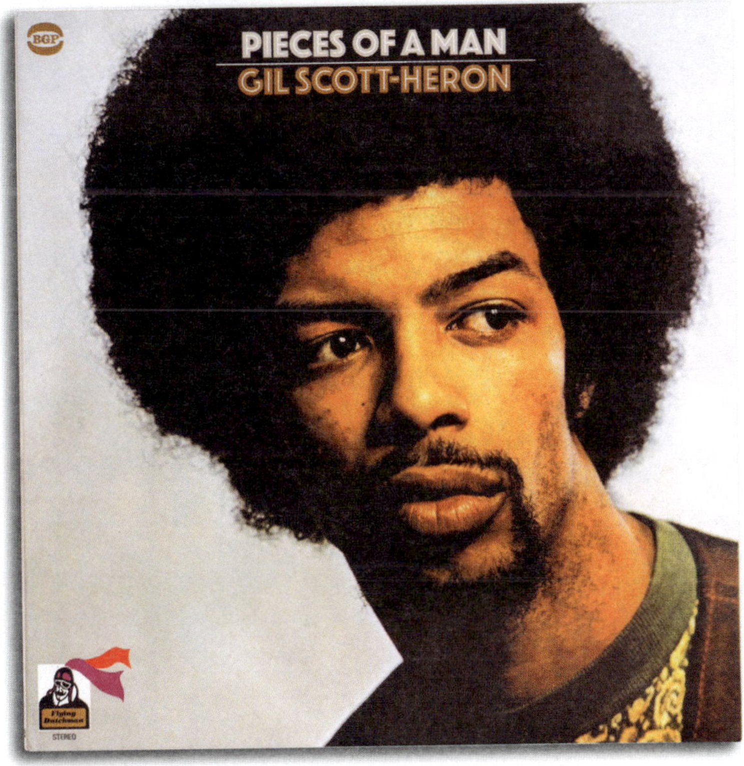

† May 27th, 2011
New York City

Gil Scott-Heron
Pieces Of A Man
Flying Dutchman, 1971
Haig Adishian (Design)
Charles Stewart (Photo)

27 MAY

* May 28th, 1944
Gladys Maria Knight
Atlanta (Georgia)

Gladys Knight & The Pips
Silk N' Soul
Soul, 1968
Cover Artists Unknown

28   MAY

* May 29th, 1956
La Toya Yvonne Jackson
Gary (Indiana)

Janet Jackson
Control
A&M Records, 1986
Chuck Beeson (Design)
Tony Viramontes (Photo)

29 MAY

Various Artists
That's Soul 3
Atlantic Records, 1968
Johannes Heinz Löffler (Design)

30 MAY

Spinners
Yesterday Today & Tomorrow
Atlantic Records, 1977
Eric Porter (Design)
Richard J. Stanley (Photo)

31 MAY

† Jun 1st, 1991
Philadelphia (Pennsylvania)

David Ruffin
Who I Am
Motown Record Corp., 1975
Frank Mulvey (Design)
Norman Seef (Photo)

01 JUN

† Jun 2nd, 2008
Ellas McDaniel
Acher (Florida)

Bo Diddley
Big Bad Bo
Chess, 1974
Neil Terk (Design)
Hank Dunning (Photo)

02 JUN

* Jun 3rd, 1942
Curtis Lee Mayfield
Chicago (Illinois)

Curtis Mayfield
Back To The World
Curtom Records, 1973
Glen Christensen (Design)
Gary Wolkowitz (Illustration)

03 JUN

Instant Funk
The Funk Is On
Salsoul Records, 1980
Stanley Hochstadt (Design)
Ken Kaltman (Photo)

04 JUN

Various Artists
Step Inside My Soul
Cree Records, 2015
Merten Kaatz (Design)
Roland "Ole Schleef" Krieger (Illustration)

05 JUN

† Jun 6th, 2006
Billy Preston
Scottsdale (Arizona)

Billy Preston
A Whole New Thing
A&M Records, 1977
Roland Young (Design)
Moshe Brakha (Photo)

06 JUN

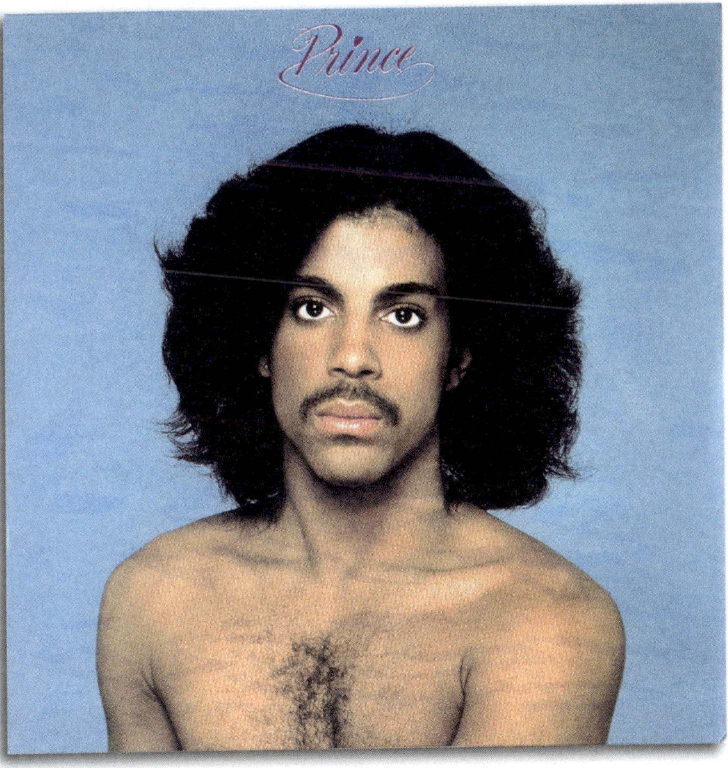

* Jun 7th, 1968
Prince Rogers Nelson
Mineapolis (Minnesota)

Prince
Warner Bros. Records, 1979
George Chacon, Lynn Barron (Design)
Jürgen Reisch (Photo)

07 JUN

Isley Jasper Isley
Caravan Of Love
Epic Records, 1985
Georgina Lehner (Design)
Gary Heery (Photo)

08 JUN

Various Artists
Invasion Funk Masters
Soul Patrol Records, 1998
Cover Artists Unknown

09 JUN

† Jun 10th, 2004
Raymond Charles Robinson
Beverly Hills (California)

Ray Charles
King Of Soul
ABC Records, Hörzu, 1968
Günther Kieser (Illustration)

10   JUN

CURTIS HARDING
FACE YOUR FEAR

* Jun 11th, 1979
Saginaw (Michigan)

Curtis Harding
Face Your Fear
Anti Records, 2017
Trevor Hernandez (Design)
Hedi Slimane (Photo)

11 JUN

Oran' Juice' Jones feat. Stu Large
Player's Call
Tommy Boy, 1997
Michelle Willems (Design)

12 JUN

* Jun 14th, 1944

Kool & The Gang
Spirit Of The Boogie
De-Lite Records, 1975
Frank Daniel (Design)
Goodnight (Illustration)

13 JUN

Linda Clifford & Curtis Mayfield
The Right Combination
RSO, 1980
Glenn Ross (Design)
Dennis Scott (Photo)

14 JUN

20 %
PREORDER DISCOUNT!

Last chance to order the new vinyl covers calendar with highest discount until June, 30th.

www.seltmannpublishers.com
Worldwide shipping, free within Germany

J. Blackfoot
City Slicker
Soundtown Records, 1983
Randy Powers (Illustration)

15 JUN

* Jun 16th, 1941
Lamont Herbert Dozier
Detroit (Michigan)

Lamont Dozier
Bittersweet
Warner Bros. Records, 1979
John Cabalka (Design)
Barry Feinstein (Photo)

16 JUN

Diana Ross & The Supremes
Let The Sunshine In
Tamla Motown, 1969
Dean O. Torrence (Design)

17 JUN

Various Artists
Studio One Soul – The Original
Soul Jazz Records, 2001
Adrian Self, Spikely Munche (Design)

18 JUN

Gabriels
Love And Hate In A Different Time
Gabriels, 2020
Cover Artists Unknown

19 JUN

The Miracles
Do It Baby
Tamla Motown, 1974
Frank Frezzo (Illustration)

20 JUN

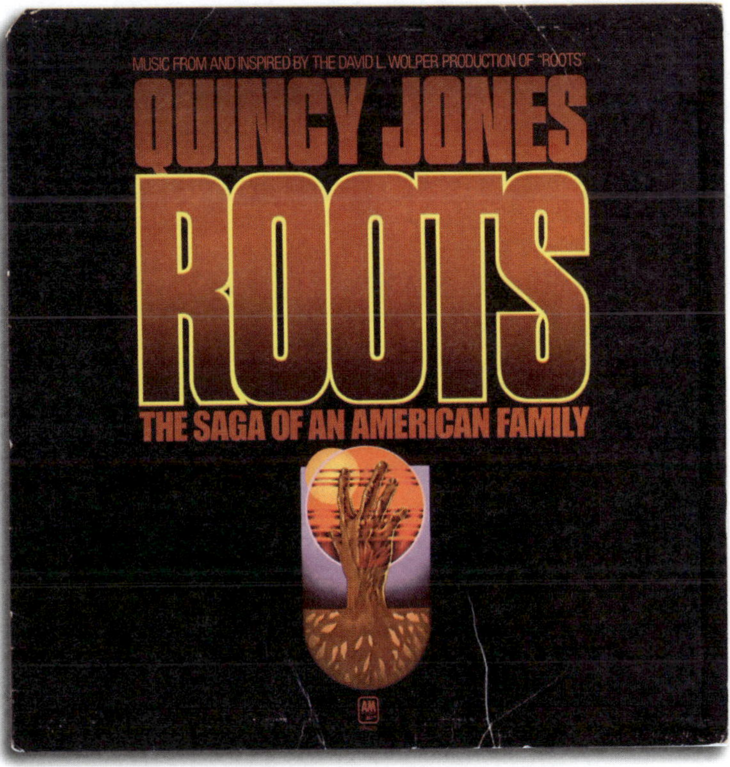

Original Motion Soundtrack – Quincy Jones
Roots – The Saga Of An American Family
A&M Records, 1977
Cover Artists Unknown

21 JUN

Angelo Bond
Bondage
ABC Records, 1975
Fred Valentine (Design)
Ron Slenzak (Photo)

22 JUN

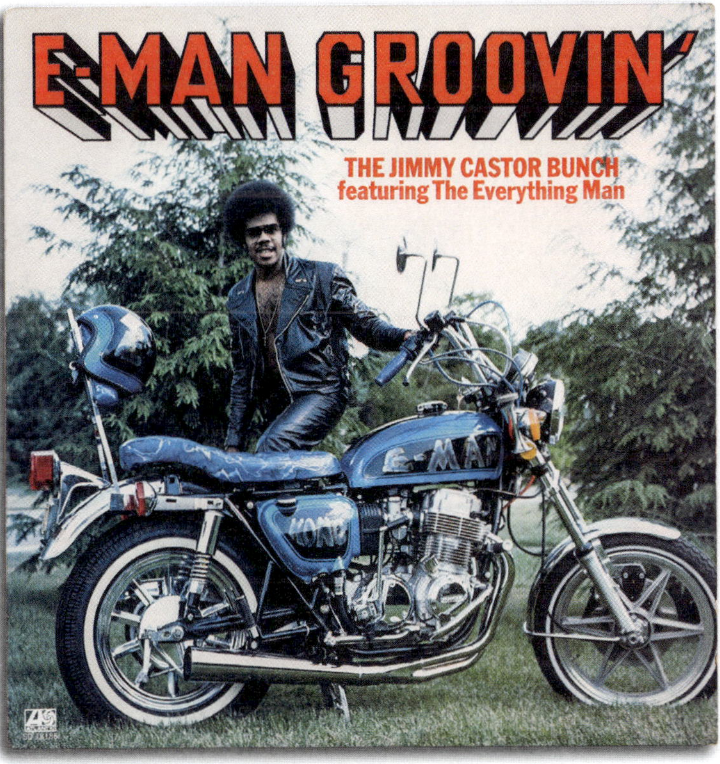

* Jun 23rd, 1940
Jimmy Castor
New York City

The Jimmy Castor Bunch
E-Man Groovin'
Atlantic Records, 1976
Kwame Braithwaite (Photo)

23   JUN

* Jun 24th, 1986
Solange Piaget Knowles
Houston (Texas)

Solange
A Seat At The Table
Columbia, 2016
Querida (Design)

24 JUN

† Jun 25th, 2009
Michael Joseph Jackson
Los Angeles (California)

Michael Jackson
Thriller
Epic Japan, 1982
Mac James (Design)
Dick Zimmermann (Photo)

25   JUN

Various Artists
Shaolin Soul Episode 4
Because Music, 2018
Uncle O (Design)
Nobuyoshi Araki (Photo)

BOBBY WOMACK

THE LAST SOUL MAN

† Jun 27th, 2014
Robert "Bobby" Dwayne Womack
Tarzana (California)

Bobby Womack
The Last Soul Man
MCA Records, 1987
Cover Artists Unknown

27   JUN

War
The World Is A Ghetto
United Artists Records, 1972
Lee Oskar (Design)
Howard Miller (Illustration)

28   JUN

Various Artists
New York Soul '66
History of Soul, 2017
Cover Artists Unknown

29 JUN

* Jun 30th, 1951
Philadelphia (Pennsylvania)

Stanley Clarke
School Days
Nemperor Records, 1976
Bob Defrin, Lynn Breslin (Design)
Robert Giusti (Illustration)

30 JUN

* Jul 1st, 1936
Holy Springs (Mississippi)

Syl Johnson
Dresses Too Short
Twinight Records, 1968
Jerry Griffith (Design)

01 JUL

The S.O.S. Band
S.O.S. III
Tabu Records, 1982
Jones & Armitage (Design)
Diem Jones (Photo)

02 JUL

Various Artists
A Treasure Chest Of Northern Soul
V.O.R., 1999
Cover Artists Unknown

03 JUL

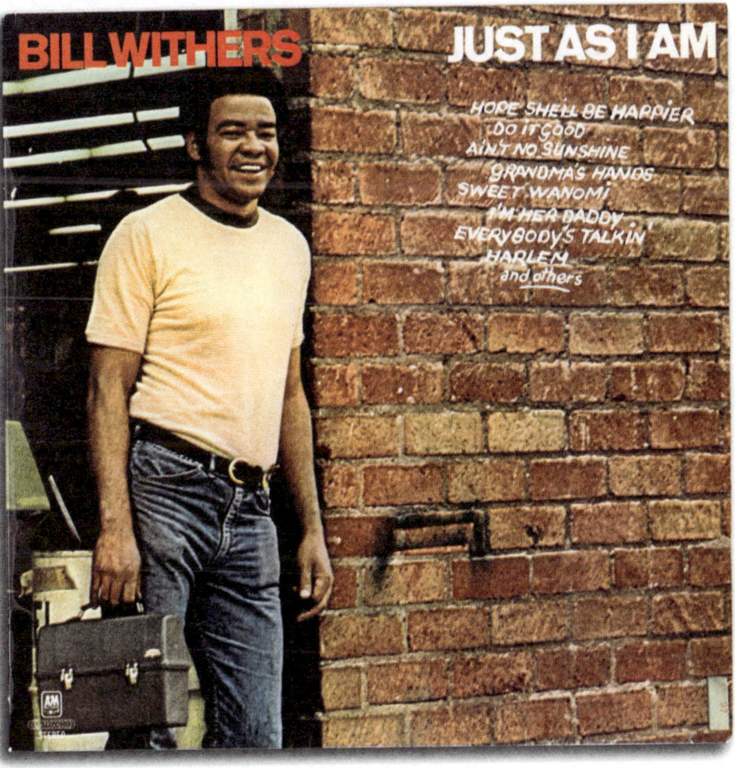

* Jul 4th, 1938
William Harrison Withers
Slab Fork (West Virginia)

Bill Withers
Just As I Am
A&M Records, 1971
Norbert Jobst (Photo)

04 JUL

The Neville Brothers
Yellow Moon
A&M Records, 1989
Jeff Gold (Design)
Tony Fitzpatrick (Illustration)

05 JUL

Graham Central Station
Release Yourself
Warner Bros. Records, 1974
Larry Graham (Design)
Mike Salisbury (Photo)

06 JUL

The Temptations
1990
Tamla Motown, 1973
Desmond Strobel, John Cale, Terry Squire (Design)
Jim Britt (Photo)

07 JUL

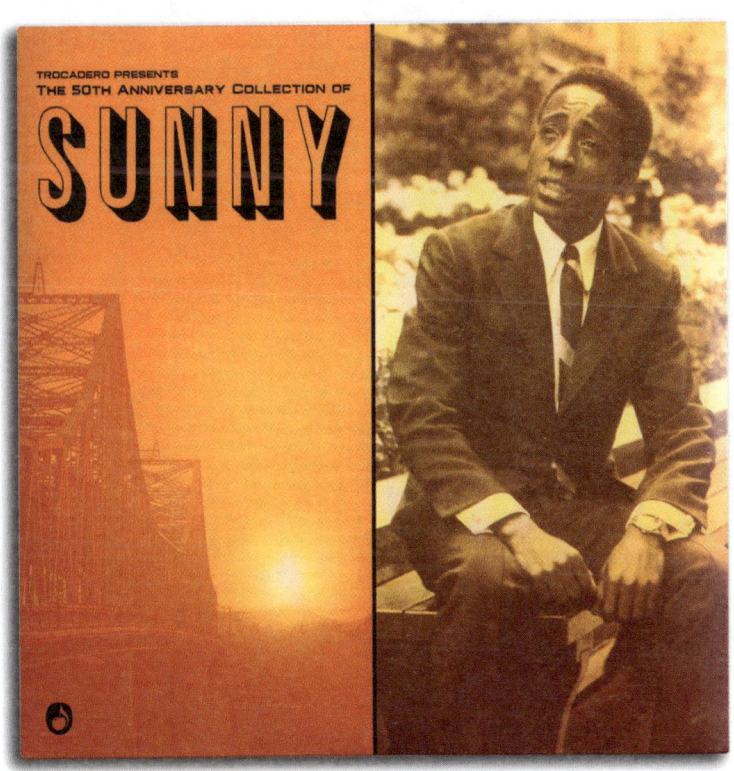

Various Artists
The 50th Anniversary Collection Of Sunny
Trocadero Records, 2016
Antje Schröder (Design)

08 JUL

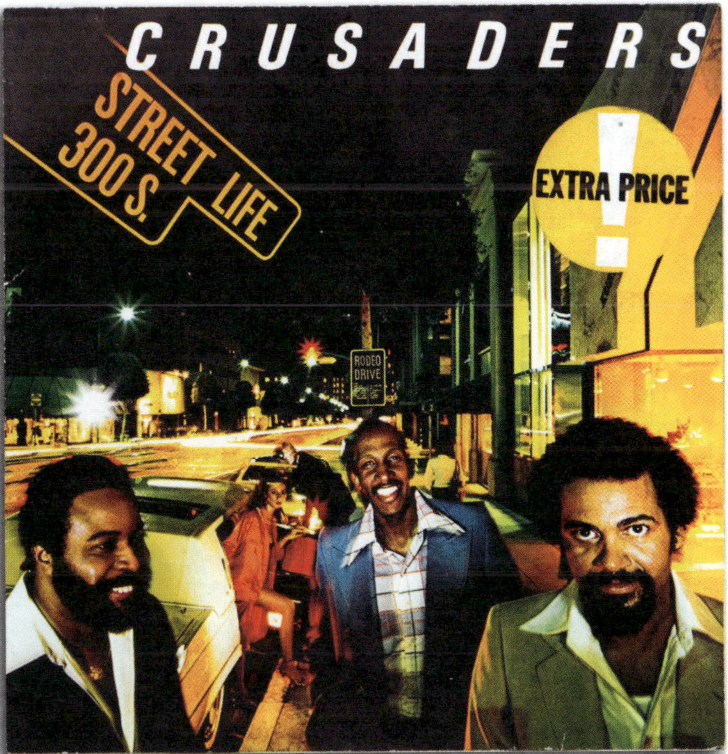

Crusaders
Street Life
MCA Records, 1979
Stuart Kusher (Design)
Jayme Odgers (Photo)

09 JUL

Jackson Five
Lookin' Through The Windows
Tamla Motown, 1972
Cover Artists Unknown

10 JUL

The Staples
Family Tree
Warner Bros. Records, 1977
Jim Ladwig (Design)
Hauser / D'Orio (Photo)

11 JUL

The Vibrations
Greatest Hits
Okeh Records, 1969
Richard Mantel (Design)

12 JUL

**Martin Freeman & Eddie Piller present
Soul On The Corner**
Acid Jazz, 2019
The Unknown (Design)
Dean Chalkley (Photo)

13 JUL

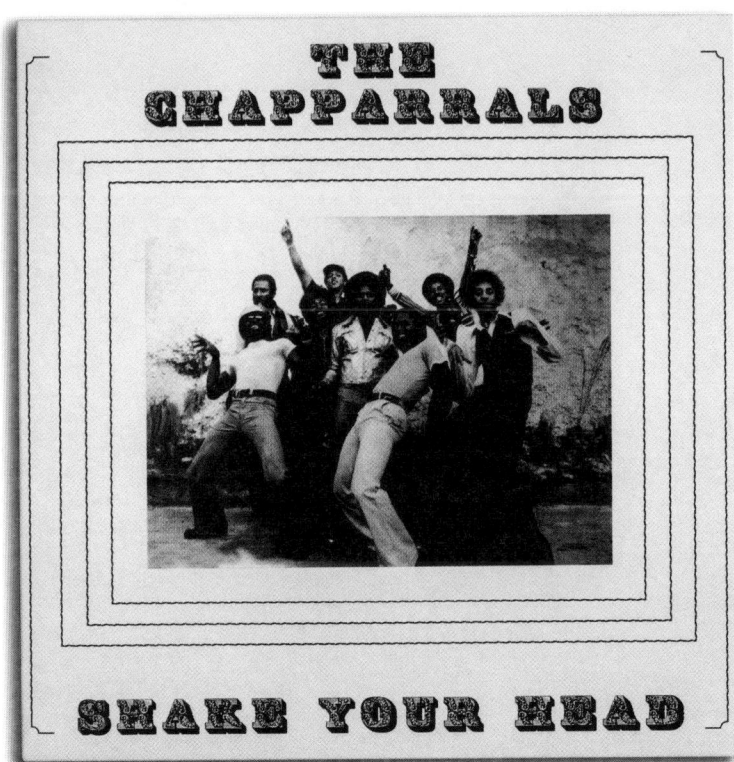

The Chapparrals
Shake Your Head
Maximillion Records Everland, 1978
Horace C. Henry (Design)

14 JUL

Millie Jackson
Hard Times
Spring Records, 1972
Bob Heimall (Design)
Tom Newson (Illustration)

15 JUL

Ohio Players
Angel
Mercury, 1977
Jim Ladwig (Design)
Victor Paul Skrebneski (Photo)

16 JUL

Mulatu Astatke & His Ethiopian Quintet
Afro-Latin Soul
Worthy Records, 1966
Cover Artists Unknown

17 JUL

Manhattans
Greatest Hits
Columbia, 1980
Cover Artists Unknown

18 JUL

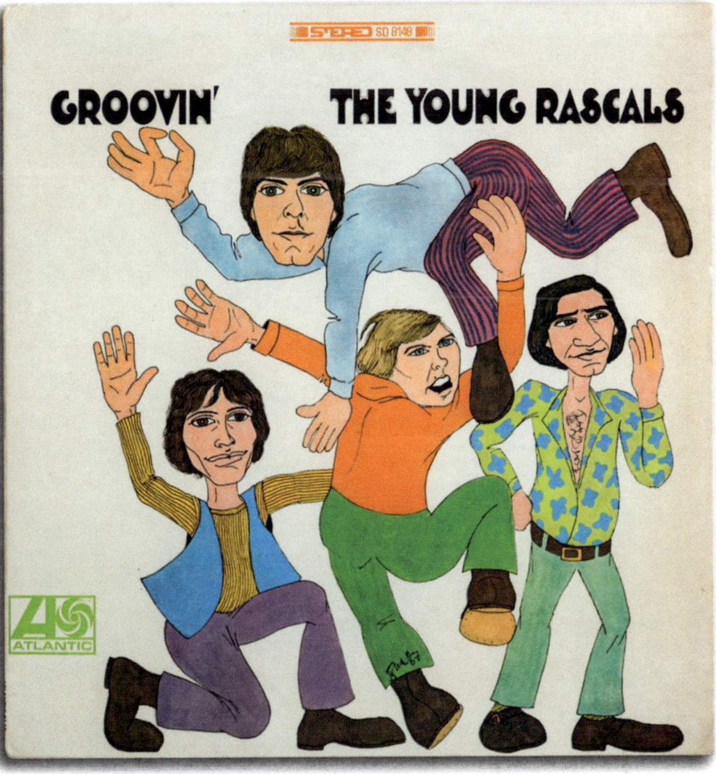

The Young Rascals
Groovin'
Atlantic, 1967
Dino Danelli (Design)
Lynn Rubin (Illustration)

19 JUL

Earth, Wind & Fire
Open Your Eyes
CBS Records, 1974
Pacific Eye & Ear (Design)
Lee Lawrence (Photo)

20 JUL

Trouble Funk
Trouble Over Here, Trouble Over There
Island Records, 1987
Tony Wright (Design)
George DuBose (Photo)

21 JUL

Dusty Springfield
Dusty in Memphis
Philips, 1969
Cover Artists Unknown

22 JUL

† Jul 23rd, 2011
Amy Jade Winehouse
London (UK)

Amy Winehouse
The Ska Collection
2Thin Records, 2014
Cover Artists Unknown

The Miracles
City Of Angeles
Tamla Motown, 1975
Frank Mulvey (Design)
Alan Bergman (Photo)

24 JUL

Marta Ren & The Groovelvets
Stop Look Listen
Record Kicks, 2016
Aloísio Brito (Photo)

25 JUL

† Jul 26th, 1992
Mary Esther Wells
Los Angeles (California)

Mary Wells
My Baby Just Cares For Me
Tamla Motown, 1965
Dezo Hoffmann (Photo)

26 JUL

Monophonics
It's Only Us
Colemine Records, 2020
Leroi Conroy (Design)
Danny Lyon & Erica Caldwell (Photo)

27 JUL

The Staples
Pass It On
Warner Bros. Records, 1976
Jim Ladwig (Design)
Richard Fegley (Photo)

28 JUL

The 5th Dimension
Earthbound
ABC Records, 1975
Carole Rubinstein (Photo)

29 JUL

Maze feat. Frankie Beverly
Live In New Orleans
Capitol Records, 1981
Cover Artists Unknown

30 JUL

The Players Association
Born To Dance
Vanguard, 1977
Jules Haflant (Design)
Frank Kulleogy (Photo)

31 JUL

Wilson Pickett
Don't Knock My Love
Atlantic, 1971
Loring Eutemey (Design)
Jim Cummins (Photo)

01 AUG

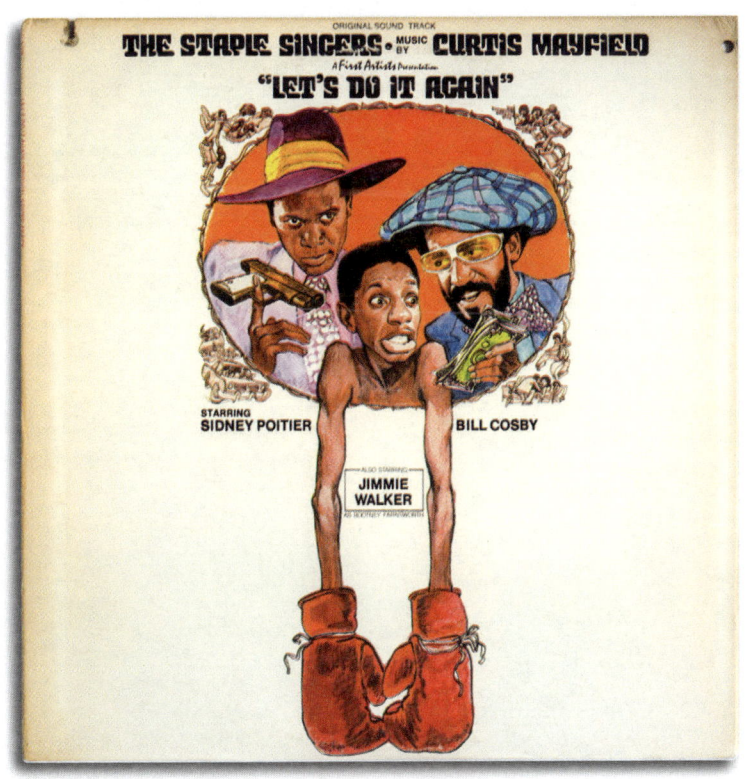

**Original Motion Soundtrack – The Staple Singers
Let's Do It Again**
Curtom Records, 1975
Bad Kanawyer (Design)
Sandy Kossin (Illustration)

02 AUG

The Dynamic Superiors
Pure Pleasure
Motown Record Corp., 1975
Frank Mulvey (Design)
Olivier Ferrand (Photo)

03 AUG

Soul II Soul
Club Classics Vol. One
10 Records, 1989
David Jones (Design)
Jamie Morgan (Photo)

04 AUG

† Aug 5th, 2013
George Duke
Los Angeles (California)

George Duke
Follow The Rainbow
Epic, 1979
Tony Lane (Design)
Bruce W. Talamon (Photo)

05 AUG

† Aug 6th, 2004
James Ambrose Johnson Junior
Los Angeles (California)

Rick James
Street Songs
Gordy, 1981
Johnny Lee (Design)
Ron Slenzak (Photo)

06 AUG

† Aug 7th, 1984
Esther Mae Jones
Los Angeles (California)

Esther Philipps
Alone Again, Naturally
Kudu Records, 1972
Bob Ciano (Design)
Mort Mace (Photo)

07 AUG

† Aug 8th, 2022
Lamont Herbert Dozier
Scottsdale (Arizona)

Lamont Dozier
Bittersweet
Warner Bros. Records, 1978
John Cabalka (Design)
Barry Feinstein (Photo)

08 AUG

* Aug 9th, 2000
Anaïs Oluwatoyin Estelle Marinho
London (UK)

Arlo Parks
Collapsed In Sunbeams
Transgressive Records, 2021
Matt de Jong (Design)
Jack Bridgland (Photo)

09 AUG

† Aug 10th, 2008
Isaac Lee Hayes, Jr.
Memphis (Tennessee)

Isaac Hayes
In The Beginning
Atlantic Records, 1972
Stanislaw Zagorski (Design)

10 AUG

Rufus feat. Chaka Khan
Rags To Rufus
ABC Records, 1974
Arthur Lee Hanson (Photo)

11 AUG

Booker T. And The M.G.'s
Soul Limbo
Stax Records, 1968
Christopher Whorf (Design)
George Whiteman (Photo)

12 AUG

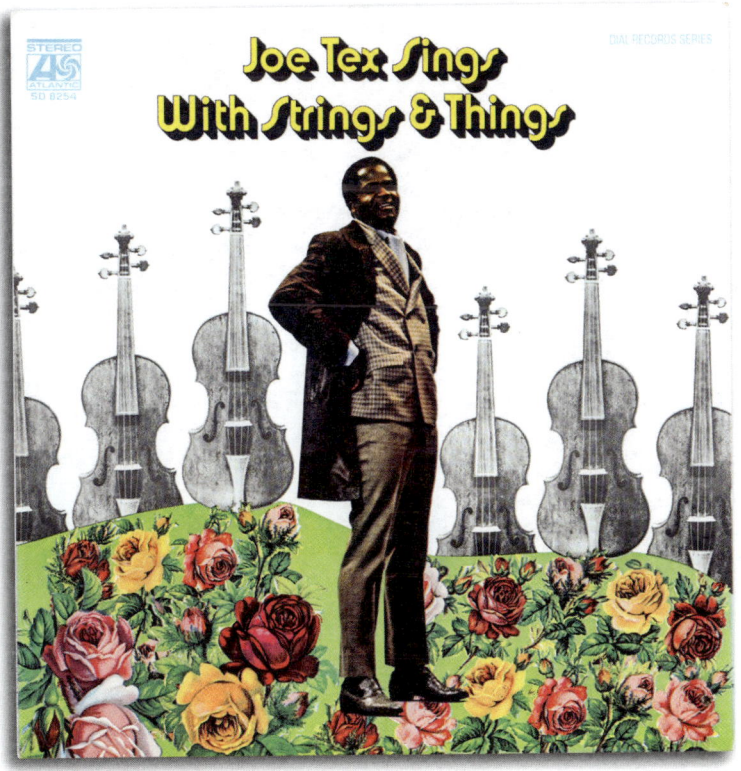

† Aug 13th, 1982
Navasota (Texas)

Joe Tex
Joe Tex Sings With Strings & Things
Atlantic, 1970
Loring Eutemey (Design)
Joel Brodsky (Photo)

13 AUG

Various Artists
Can You Feel The Beat (Funky 45s & Other Rare Groove)
J & D, 2016
Steve Jaffa (Design)

* Aug 15th, 1934
Toccoa, Georgia

Bobby Byrd & The J.B.'S All Stars
Finally Getting Paid
Rhythm Attack Productions, 1988
Chica Walderdorff, Marika Zwick (Design)
Wolfgang Burat (Photo)

15 AUG

The Nite-Liters
Different Strokes
RCA Victor, 1972
Acy Lehman (Design)

16 AUG

Various Artists
More Dirty Laundry – The Soul Of Black Country
Trikont Records, 2008
Hias Schaschko (Design)

17 AUG

Original Soundtrack – The Impressions
Three The Hard Way
Curtom Records, 1974
Reggie Morrison (Design)

18 AUG

* Aug 19th, 1940
John Lester Nash Jr.
Houston (Texas)

Johnny Nash
Soul Folk
JAD, 1969
Jack Lohshein (Design)

19 AUG

* Aug 20th, 1942
Isaac Lee Hayes, Jr.
Covington (Tennessee)

Isaac Hayes
Joy
Stax Records, 1973
Ron Gordon (Design)
Ken Marcus (Photo)

20 AUG

* Aug 21st, 1979
Kelis Rogers
Harlem (New York City)

Kelis
Food
Ninja Tune, 2014
Kate Moross (Design)
Leif Podhajsky (Photo)

21 AUG

* Aug 22nd, 1936
Charles Louis Brown
Gaston (North Catrolina)

Chuck Brown and The Soul Searchers
Live-D.C. Bumpin' Y'All
Flame Records, 1987
Fiona Hawthorne (Illustration)

22 AUG

Mayer Hawthorne
How Do You Do
Universal, 2009
Mayer Hawthorne (Design)
Cedric Bihr (Photo)

23 AUG

Original Soundtrack by Isaac Hayes
Tough Guys
Enterprise Records, 1974
The Stax Organisation (Design)

24 AUG

JAN DELAY

WIR KINDER VOM BAHNHOF SOUL

* Aug 25th, 1976
Jan Philipp Eißfeld
Hamburg (Germany)

Jan Delay
Wir Kinder vom Bahnhof Soul
Buback, 2009
Felix Schlüter (Design)
Gulliver Theis (Photo)

25 AUG

Funkadelic
Hardcore Jollies
Warner Bros. Records, 1976
Bob Krasnow (Design)

26 AUG

Smokey Robinson
Pure Smokey
Tamla Motown, 1974
Bob Gleason (Design)
Jim Britt (Photo)

27 AUG

Various Artists
The Smoocher
Big Cheese Records, 1994
Lazoo (Illustration)

28 AUG

* Aug 29th, 1958
Michael Joseph Jackson
Gary (Indiana)

Michael Jackson
Off The Wall
Epic Records, 1979
Mike Salisbury (Design)
Steve Harvey (Photo)

29 AUG

JAMES MASON
RHYTHM OF LIFE

James Mason
Rhythm Of Life
Chiaroscuro Records, 1977
Ron Warwell (Design)
Rollo Phlecks (Photo)

30 AUG

Bloodstone
Unreal
London Records, 1973
Vincent Biondi (Design)
Jeffrey Weisel (Photo)

31 AUG

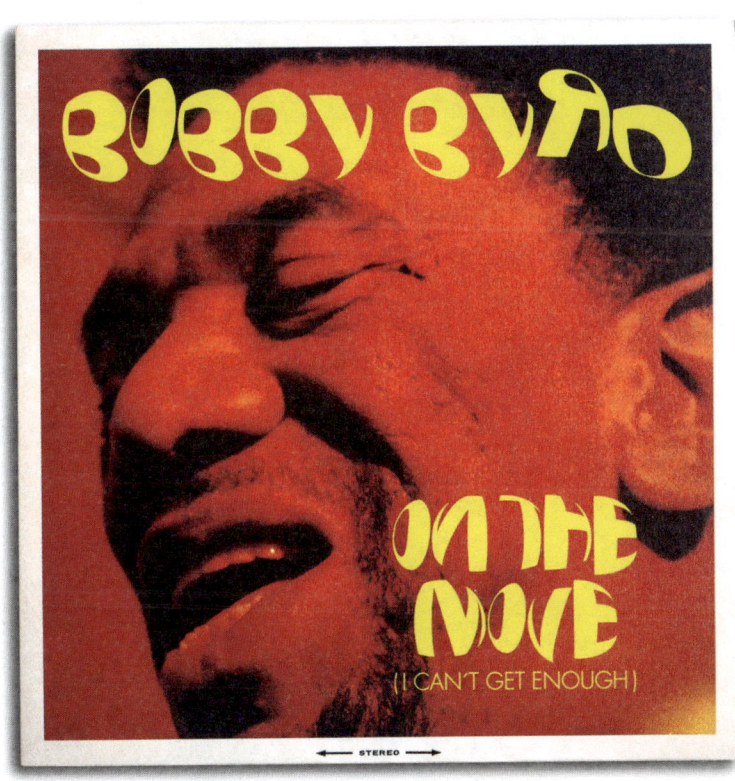

Bobby Byrd
On The Move (I Can't Get Enough)
Soulciety Records, 1993
Soulciety, Tim Krink (Design)
Björn Lux (Photo)

01 SEP

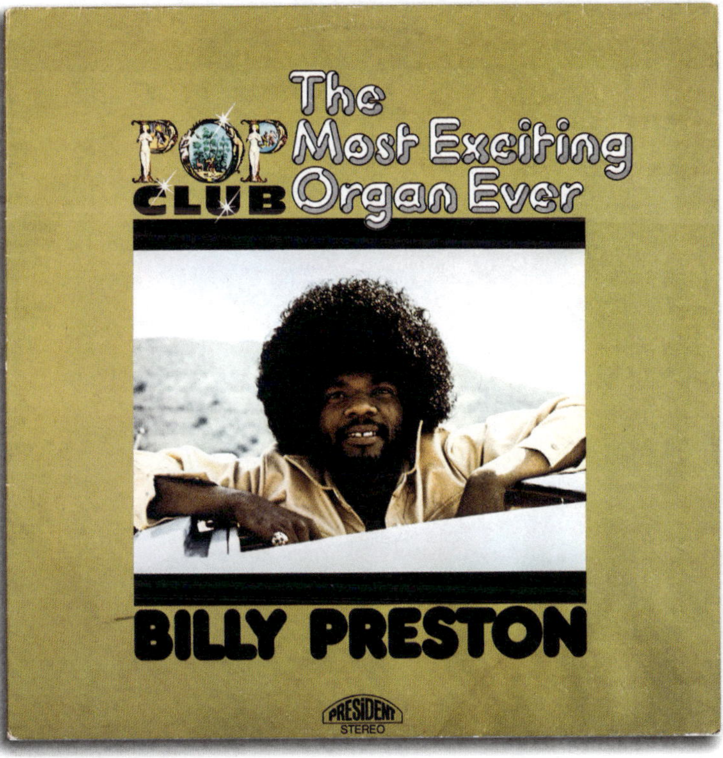

The Most Exciting Organ Ever

POP CLUB

BILLY PRESTON

* Sep 2nd, 1946
Billy Preston
Houston (Texas)

Billy Preston
The Most Exciting Organ Ever
President Records, 1968
Cover Artists Unknown

02 SEP

Durand Jones & The Indications
Private Space
Dead Oceans, 2021
Miles Johnson (Design)
Ebru Yildiz (Photo)

03 SEP

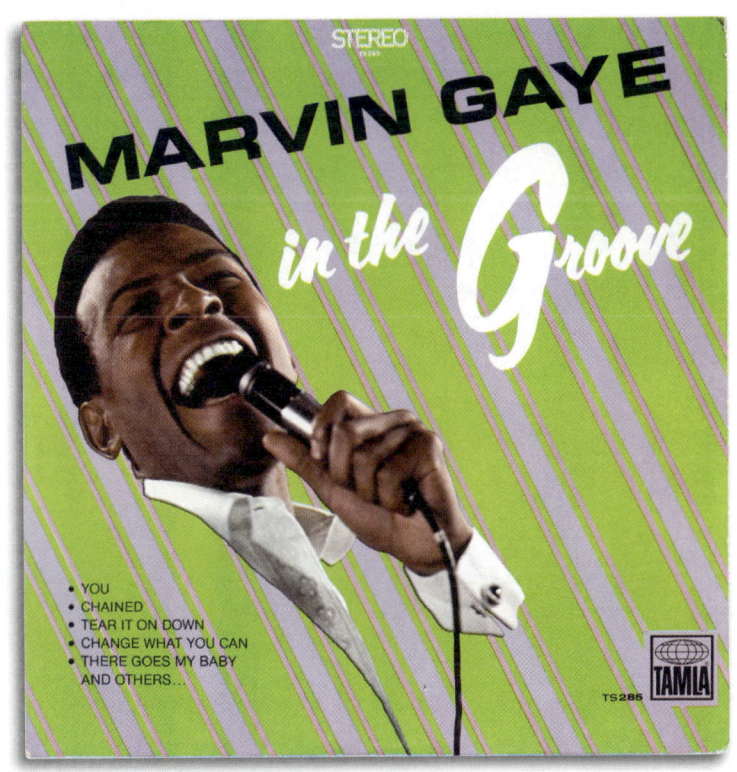

Marvin Gaye
In The Groove
Tamla Motown, 1968
Herbart (Design)
Motown GA-P. Bass (Photo)

04 SEP

The Jimmy Castor Bunch
Maximum Stimulation
Atlantic Records, 1977
Jimmy Castor, John Pruitt (Design)

05 SEP

Original Soundtrack – Roy Ayers
Coffy
Polydor, 1973
Vartan Kurjian (Design)

06 SEP

Various Artists
Tamla-Motown Is Hot, Hot, Hot Vol. 3
Tamla Motown, 1965
Cover Artists Unknown

07 SEP

Grover Washington Jr.
Winelight
Elektra, 1980
Ron Coro (Design)
Jim Shea (Photo)

08 SEP

* Sep 9th, 1941
Otis Redding
Dawson (Georgia)

Otis Redding
The Soul Album
Volt Records, 1966
Loring Euterney (Design)
Peter Levy (Photo)

09 SEP

* Sep 10th, 1940
Roy Edward Ayers
Los Angeles (California)

Roy Ayers
Let's Do It
Polydor, 1978
Dick Zimmermann (Photo)

10 SEP

Afrika Gumbe
Estúdio Eldorado, 1989
Sergio Chataigner (Design)
Tasso Pessurno (Illustration)

11 SEP

* Sep 12th, 1944
Barry Eugene White
Galveston (Texas)

The Love Unlimited Orchestra
Rhapsody In White
20th Century Records, 1974
Mark Weinberg (Design)

12 SEP

Booker T. & M.G.'s
Melting Pot
Stax Records, 1970
Stan Hochstadt, The Graffiteria (Design)
George Rodriguez (Photo)

13 SEP

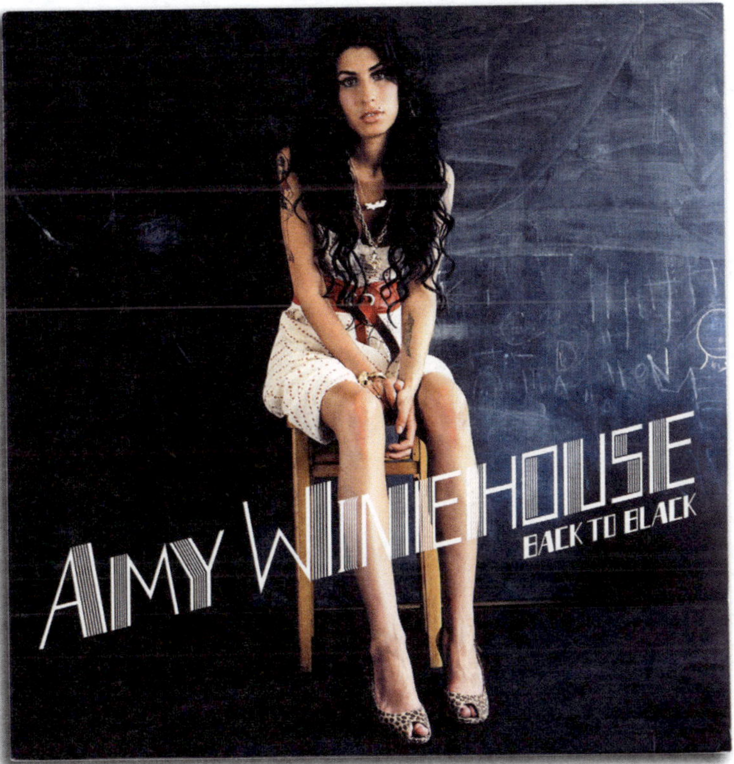

* Sep 14th, 1983
Amy Jade Winehouse
Southgate (London)

Amy Winehouse
Back To Black
Universal Records, 2007
Alex Hutchinson & Free Barrabas! (Design)
Mischa Richter (Photo)

14 SEP

Various Artists
Rocksteady Got Soul
Soul Jazz Records, 2021
Adrian Self & Duke Tueday (Design)

15 SEP

Alex Brown
In Search Of Love
Everland / Sundi Records, 1970
Carl Grainger (Design)
William R. Eastabrook Photography (Photo)

16 SEP

Original Soundtrack
Shaft
Stax Records, 1971
Tony Seiniger (Design)

17 SEP

Various Artists
Mojo Club Presents Dancefloor Jazz Vol. Two
Polydor, 1993
Marion Schnelle, Matthias Lemcke (Design)

18 SEP

† Sep 19th, 2005
Willie McKinley Hutchinson
Dallas (Texas)

Willie Hutch
Season For Love
RCA / Be With Records, 1970
Peter Whorf Graphics (Photo)

19 SEP

Sly & The Family Stone
Back To The Right Track
Warner Bros. Records, 1979
Peter Whorf (Design)
Ron Slenzak (Photo)

20 SEP

**Various Artists – Miche
With Love Volume 1**
Mr. Bongo, 2022
Sofia Bastos (Design)

21 SEP

Roberta Flack & Donny Hathaway
Atlantic Records, 1972
Jeffrey Blue (Photo)

22 SEP

The Temptations
Surface Thrills
Motown Records, 1983
Johnny Lee (Design)
Ron Slenzak (Photo)

23 SEP

Original Soundtrack – Galt MacDermot
Cotton Comes To Harlem
United Artists, 1970
Frank Gauna (Design)
Bob McGinnis (Illustration)

24 SEP

The Supremes
Where Did Yor Love Go
Motown Record Corp., 1964
Yesnin / Mead (Design)

25 SEP

Dexys Midnight Runners
Searching For Young Soul Rebels
Odeon, 1980
Fly By Night (Design)

26 SEP

Joe Simon
Happy Birthday, Baby
Spring Records, 1979
Bob Heimall (Design)
Benno Friedman (Photo)

27 SEP

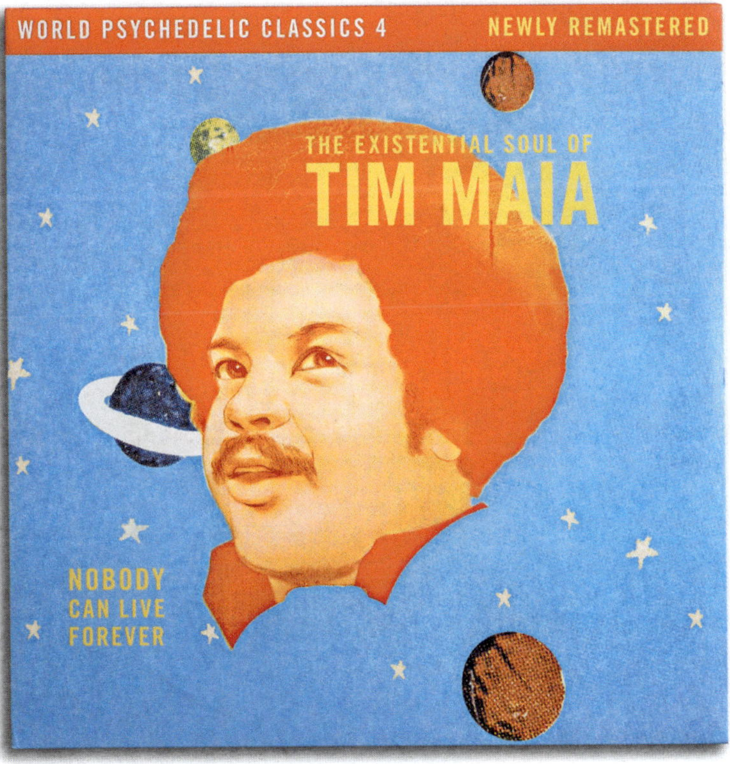

* Sep 28th, 1942
Sebastião Rodrigues Maia
Rio de Janeiro (Brazil)

Tim Maia
The Essential Soul Of Tim Maia –
Nobody Can Live Forever
Luaka Bop, 2012
Rodrigo Corral (Design)
Sam Weber (Illustration)

28 SEP

† Sep 29th, 1984
Vernon Davis
Dallas (Texas)

Geater Davis
Sweet Woman's Love
Santo Records / Bear Family, 1971
Lynda Cross (Design)

29 SEP

Jackson Five
Goin' Back To Indiana
Tamla Motown, 1971
Larry Raphael (Photo)

30 SEP

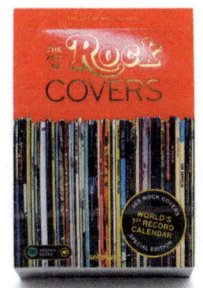
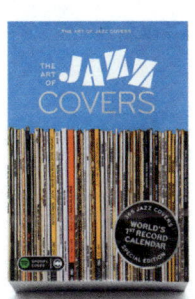

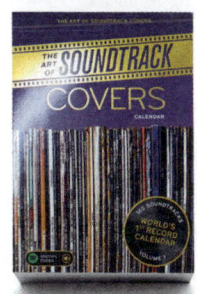
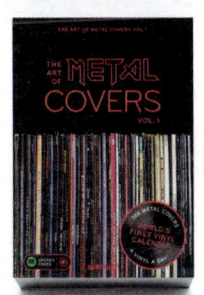

www.seltmannpublishers.com

Worldwide shipping, free within Germany

* Oct 1st, 1945
Donny Hathaway
Chicago (Illinois)

Donny Hathaway
Everything Is Everything
ATCO Records, 1970
Haig Adishian (Design)
Jim Taylor (Photo)

01 OCT

* Oct 2nd, 1962
Neil James Huntsman
Colchester (England)

James Hunter Six
Nick Of Time
Daptone Records, 2020
Ann Coombs (Design)
Jesse Perez Huntsman (Photo)

02 OCT

Skyy
Skyyport
Salsoul Record Corp., 1980
Jim O'Connell (Design)
Marlis Matews (Photo)

03 OCT

Various Artists
Soul: Groovy Anthems By The Kings Of Soul
Wagram Music, 2023
Supercinq (Design)
H. Armstrong Roberts (Photo)

04 OCT

† Oct 5th, 1992
Edward James Kendrick
Birmingham (Alabama)

Eddie Kendricks
Vintage '78
Arista Records, 1978
Hal Davis (Photo)

05 OCT

Jamila Woods
Heavn
Jagjaguwar, 2017
Swopes (Design)
Bradley Murray (Photo)

06 OCT

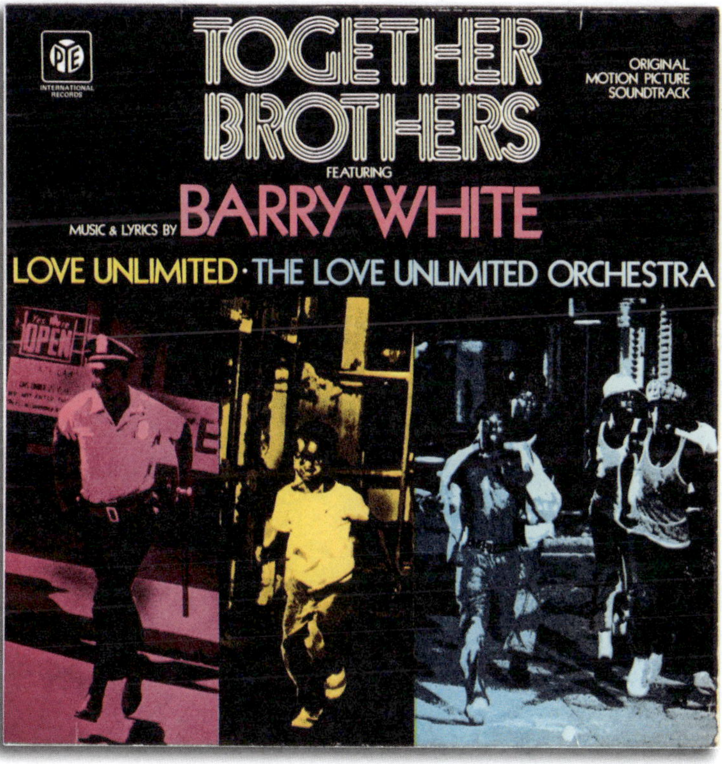

Original Motion Soundtrack – Barry White
Together Brothers
20th Century Records, 1974
Jack Levy (Design)

07 OCT

Original Motion Soundtrack – Don Julian
Savage
Money Records, 1973
Jerrold P. Woods (Design)
Marvin Rand Studios (Illustration)

08 OCT

Maze feat. Frankie Beverly
Live In New Orleans
Capitol Records, 1981
Ray Kohara (Design)
Todd Gray (Photo)

09 OCT

Various Artists
Hamburg Soul Weekender – Selected Soul Spins 2007–2019
Légère Recordings, 2019
Kerstin Holzwarth (Design)

10 OCT

Bootsy's Rubber Band
Strechin' Out In Bootsy's Rubber Band
Warner Bros. Records, 1976
Ed Trasher (Design)
George Whiteman (Photo)

11 OCT

Mandrill
Just Outside Of Town
Polydor, 1973
Ron Nackman (Design)
Don Anderson (Photo)

12 OCT

† Oct 13th, 2010
General Norman Johnson May
Atlanta (Georgia)

General Johnson
Arista Records, 1976
Nancy Greenberg (Design)
Benno Friedmann (Photo)

13 OCT

Various Artists
That's Soul II
Metronome, 1968
J.H. Löffler (Design)

14 OCT

Original Soundtrack – Marvin Gaye
Trouble Man
Tamla Motown, 1972
Cover Artists Unknown

15 OCT

Curtis Mayfield
Sweet Exorcist
Curtom Records, 1974
Milton Sincoff (Design)
Bill Ronalds (Illustration)

16 OCT

The Masqueraders
Love Anonymous
ABC Records, 1977
Stan Everson (Design)

17 OCT

The Supremes & The Four Tops
The Return Of The Magnificent Seven
Motown, 1971
Cover Artists Unknown

18 OCT

Funkadelic
Maggot Brain
Westbound Records, 1971
David Krieger (Design)
Joel Brodsky (Photo)

19 OCT

Smokey Robinson & The Miracles
Time Out
Tamla Motown, 1969
Cover Artists Unknown

20 OCT

Donnie Burks
The Swinging Sound Of Soul
Europa Records, 1969
Cover Artists Unknown

21 OCT

The American Breed
Lonely Side Of The City
Acta Records, 1968
Christopher Whorf (Design)
Sue McCartney (Photo)

22 OCT

Brass Construction
United Artists Records, 1975
Flashmaurer Productions, Mike Mendel (Design)
Jeremiah Bean (Photo)

23 OCT

Roberta Flack
Quiet Fire
Atlantic Records, 1971
Ira Friedlander (Design)
Rod Bristow (Photo)

24 OCT

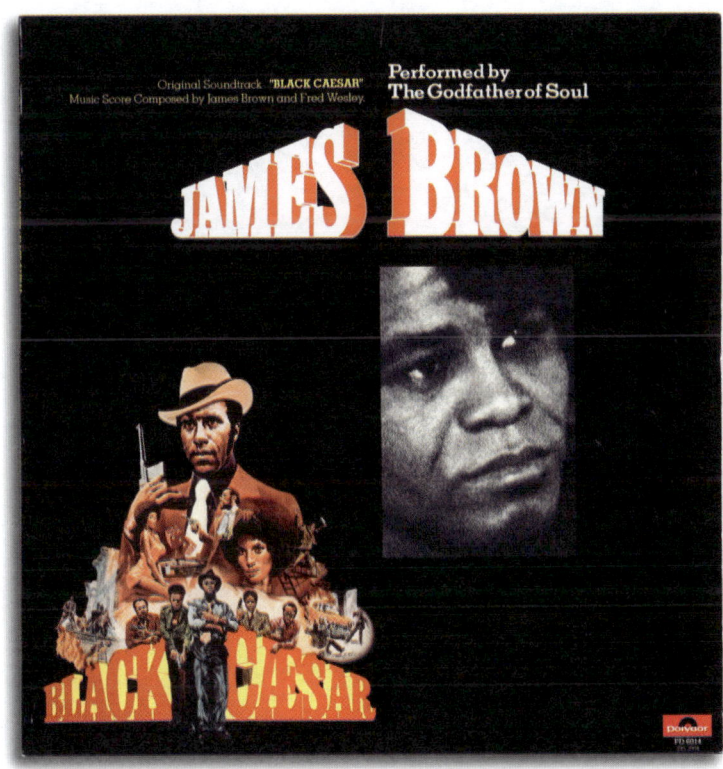

Original Motion Soundtrack – James Brown
Black Caesar
Polydor, 1973
Charles Robbit (Design)
Haywood E. Moore (Photo)

25 OCT

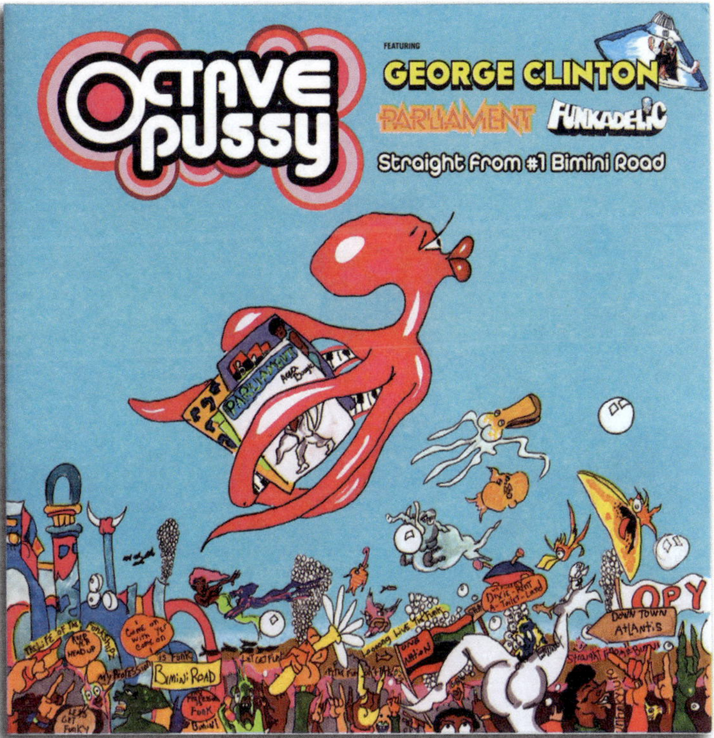

Octavepussy feat. George Clinton, Parliament
Straight From #1 Bimini Road
Tonefloat, 2019
Curtis Wilcox (Design)
Sebastian Neckel (Illustration)

26 OCT

Various Artists
Twin Cities Funk & Soul 1964–1979
Secret Stash Records, 2012
Eric Foss (Design)
Mike Zerby (Photo)

27 OCT

† Oct 28th, 1970
James T. Ramey
Chicago (Illinois)

The Baby Huey Story
The Living Legendy
Curtom Records, 1971
Michael Mendel (Design)
Gil Ross (Photo)

28 OCT

Various Artists
Black Music
Arcade Records, 1974
Cover Artists Unknown

29 OCT

Erykah Badu
Mama's Gun
Motown, Music on Vinyl, 2000
Erykah Badu, Mickey Whitfield (Design)
Robert Maxwell (Photo)

30   OCT

Halloween

Hot Blood
Dracula And Co
Carrere, 1977
Jay Palenka (Design)
George Reztips (Photo)

31 OCT

 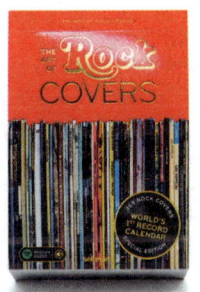 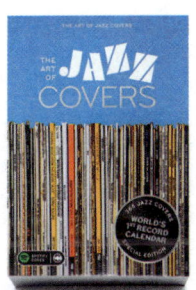
 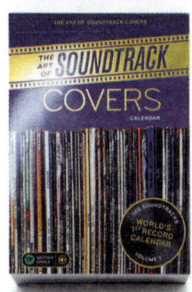 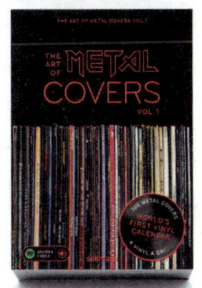
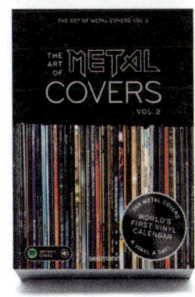  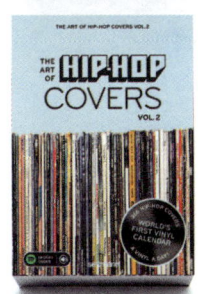

www.seltmannpublishers.com
Worldwide shipping, free within Germany

Mandrill
Polydor, 1971
Ron Nackman (Design)
Jordan Malek (Photo)

01 NOV

Maze feat. Frankie Beverly
We Are One
Capitol Records, 1983
Roy Kohara (Design)
Tito Salomoni (Illustration)

02 NOV

Roy Ayers
You Might Be Surprised
CBS Records, 1985
Cover Artists Unknown

03 NOV

The Isley Brothers
Tamla Motown Presents
Tamla Motown, 1972
Terry Beard (Design)

04 NOV

† Nov 5th, 1996
Los Angeles (California)

Eddie Harris & Les McCann
Second Movement
Atlantic Records, 1971
Alyse Koylan, Stanislaw Zagorski (Design)

05 NOV

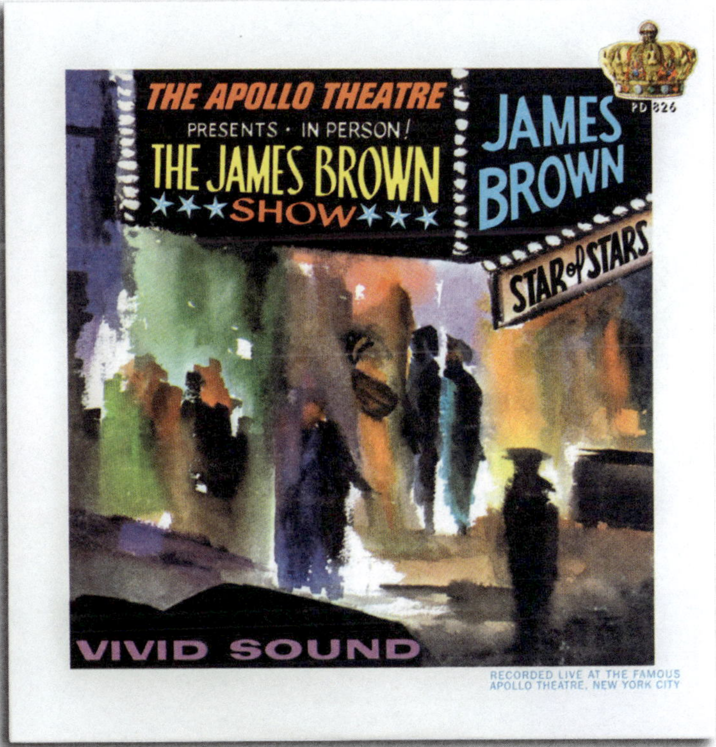

James Brown
The James Brown Show (Live At The Apollo)
King Records, 1963
Dan Quest (Illustration)

06 NOV

† Nov 7th, 2020
Cándido Camera de Guerra
New York City

Candido
Thousand Finger Man
Solid State Records, 1970
Frank Gauna (Design)
Chuck Stewart (Photo)

07   NOV

*Nov 8th, 1944
Bonnie Lynn O' Farrell
Granite City (Illinois)

**Delaney & Bonnie
D & B Together**
Columbia, 1972
John Berg (Design)
David Gahr (Photo)

08 NOV

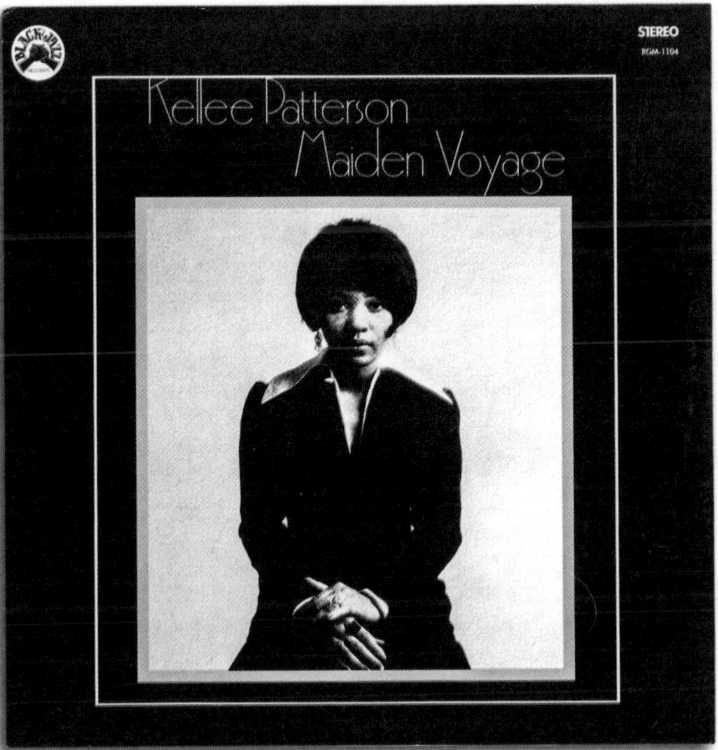

Kellee Patterson
Maiden Voyage
Black Jazz Records, 1973
PGM, Chicago (Design)
Bud Doty (Photo)

09 NOV

† Nov 10th, 1990
Philadelphia (Pennsylvannia)

Ronnie Dyson
If The Shoe Fits
Columbia, 1979
Andrea Klein, John Berg (Design)
Duane Michaels (Photo)

10 NOV

B.T. Express
Energy To Burn
Columbia, 1976
Sid Maurer (Design)
Don Hunstein (Photo)

11 NOV

The Jimmy Castor Brunch
Butt Of Course...
Atlantic Records, 1974
John Pruitt (Design)

12 NOV

† Nov 13th, 2016
Leon Russell
Nashville (Tennessee)

Leon & Mary Russell
Wedding Mum
Paradise Records, 1976
Lockart (Design)
Greg Gorman (Photo)

13   NOV

The Ikettes
Fine Fine Fine
Kent Records, 1987
Neil Watkinson (Design)
Ted Carroll (Photo)

14 NOV

The Jacksons
Victory
Epic, 1984
Michael Whelan (Illustration)

15 NOV

Sampha
Process
Young Turks, 2016
Ben Walker (Design)
Ben Walker (Photo)

16 NOV

The Untouchables
Wild Child
Stiff Records, 1985
Simon Flower (Illustration)

17 NOV

† Nov 18th, 2016
Sharon Lafaye Jones
Cooperstown (New York)

Sharon Jones & The Dap Kings
I Learned The Hard Way
Daptone Records, 2010
Ann Coombs, David Serre (Design)
Jakob Blickenstaff (Photo)

18 NOV

Superfunk
Funk Inc.
Prestige, 1973
Tony Lane (Design)

19 NOV

Original Motion Soundtrack – Mandrill / Masser / Benson
Muhammad Ali – The Greatest
Arista Records, 1977
Cover Artists Unknown

20 NOV

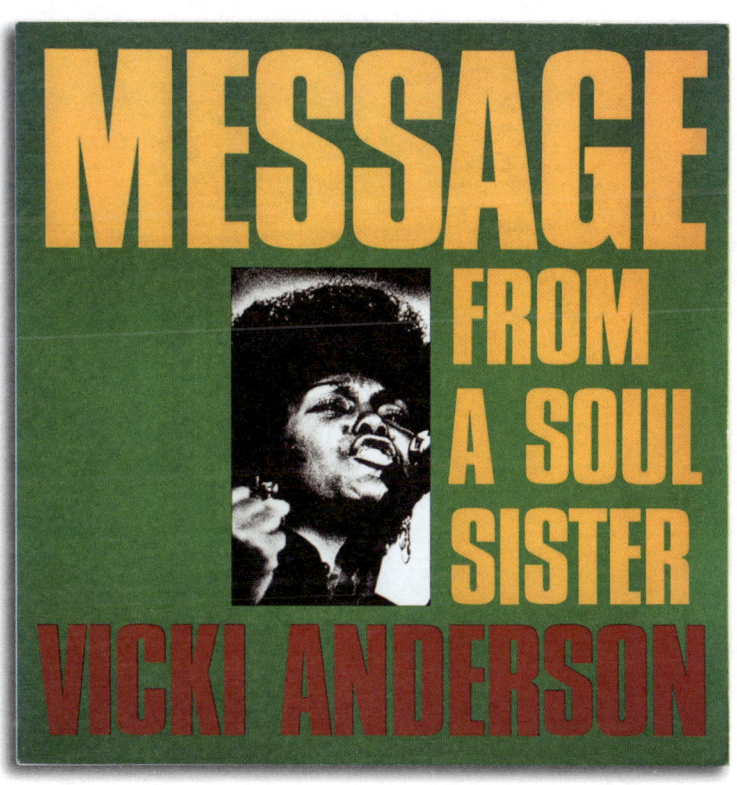

* Nov 21st, 1939
Myra Barnes
Houston (Texas)

Vicki Anderson
Message From A Soul Sister
Famous Flame Records, 1992
Cover Artists Unknown

21 NOV

Jon Hendricks
TELL ME THE TRUTH

† Nov 22nd, 2017
John Cal Hendricks
New York City

Jon Hendricks
Tell Me The Truth
Arista Records, 1975
Bob Heimall (Design)
Norman Seeff (Photo)

22 NOV

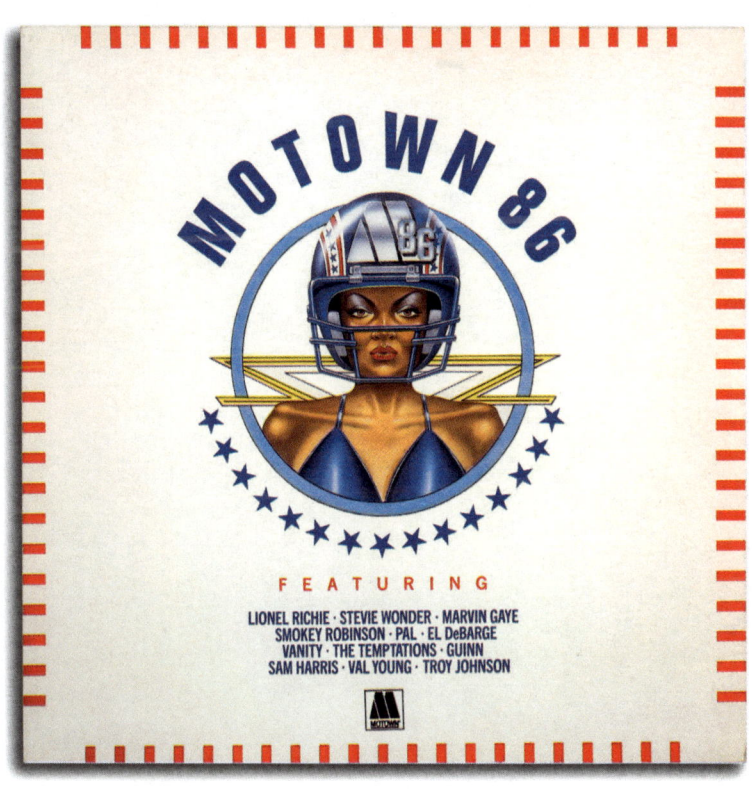

Various Artists
Motown 86
Motown Records, 1986
Cover Artists Unknown

23 NOV

15 %
BLACK WEEKEND DISCOUNT!*

Discover more calendars and other great products in our shop from Friday to Monday!

Your voucher code:

s+blck

* The only discount before the end of year! Books not included.

www.seltmannpublishers.com
Worldwide shipping, free within Germany

The Weather Girls
Success
CBS Records, 1983
Nancy Greenberg (Design)
Francesco Scavullo (Photo)

24 NOV

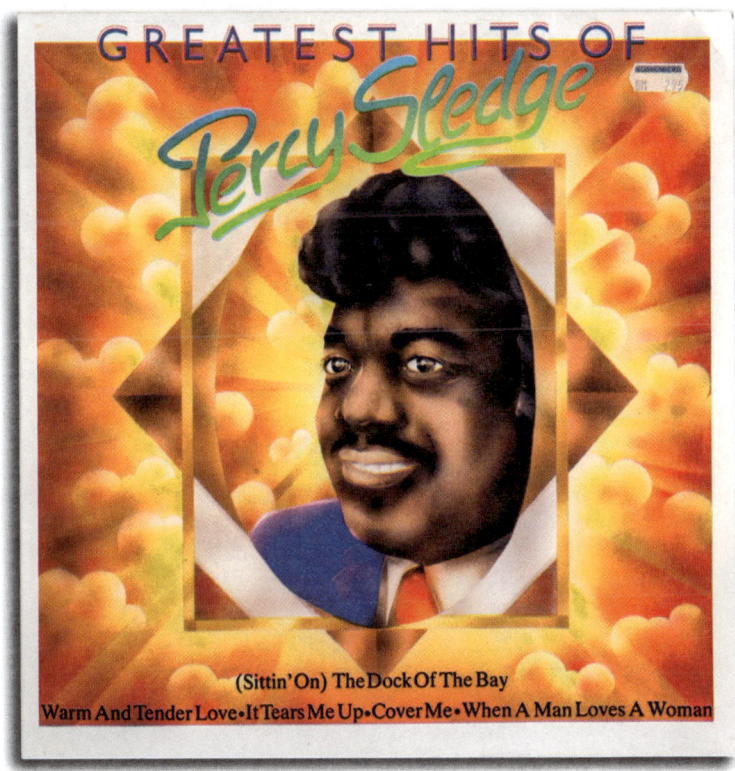

* Nov 25th, 1940
Percy Tyrone Sledge
Leighton (Alabama)

Percy Sledge
Greatest Hits Of Percy Sledge
Pentagon Records, 1987
W. Löppmann (Design)

25 NOV

* Nov 26th, 1939
Anna Mae Bullock
Brownsville (Tennessee)

Ike & Tine Turner
Nutbush City Limits
United Artists Records, 1973
Mike Salisbury (Design)
Dave Willardson (Illustration)

26 NOV

Lee Fields
My World
Truth & Soul, 2009
Danny Miller (Design)

27 NOV

Johnny Guitar Watson
A Real Mother
DJM Records, 1977
DFK, David Krieger (Design)

28 NOV

Kool & The Gang
Wild And Peaceful
Polydor, 1973
Richard Askew (Design)
Josef Askew (Illustration)

29 NOV

SHUGGIE OTIS
INSPIRATION INFORMATION

* Nov 30th, 1953
Johnny Alexander Veliotes
Los Angeles (California)

Shuggie Otis
Inspiration Information
CBS Records, 1974
John Brogna (Design)
Steven Paley (Photo)

30 NOV

Sudan Archives
Athena
Stones Throw Records, 2019
Jeff Jank, Jordi NG, Alexa Carrasco & Ben Dickey (Design)
Jack McKain (Photo)

01 DEC

The 5th Dimension
Earthbound
ABC Records, 1975
Carole Rubinstein (Illustration)

02 DEC

The Roots
The Tipping Point
Geffen Records, 2004
Gravillis Inc. (Design)
Kenny Gravillis (Photo)

03 DEC

Claudja Barry
I Wanna Be Loved By You
Lollipop Records, 1978
Eric Wuckel (Design)
Falk U. Rogner (Photo)

04 DEC

Gil Scott-Heron
Moving Target
Arista Records, 1982
Donn Davenport (Design)
John Ford (Photo)

05 DEC

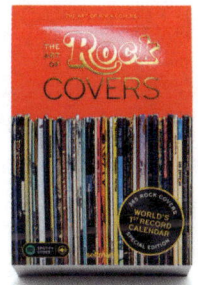
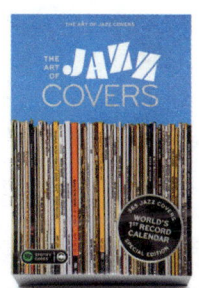

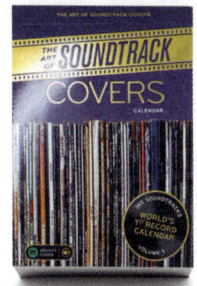
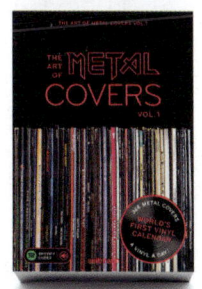
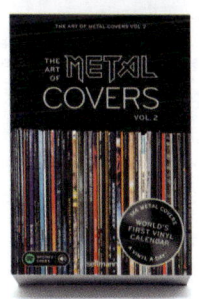

www.seltmannpublishers.com
Worldwide shipping, free within Germany

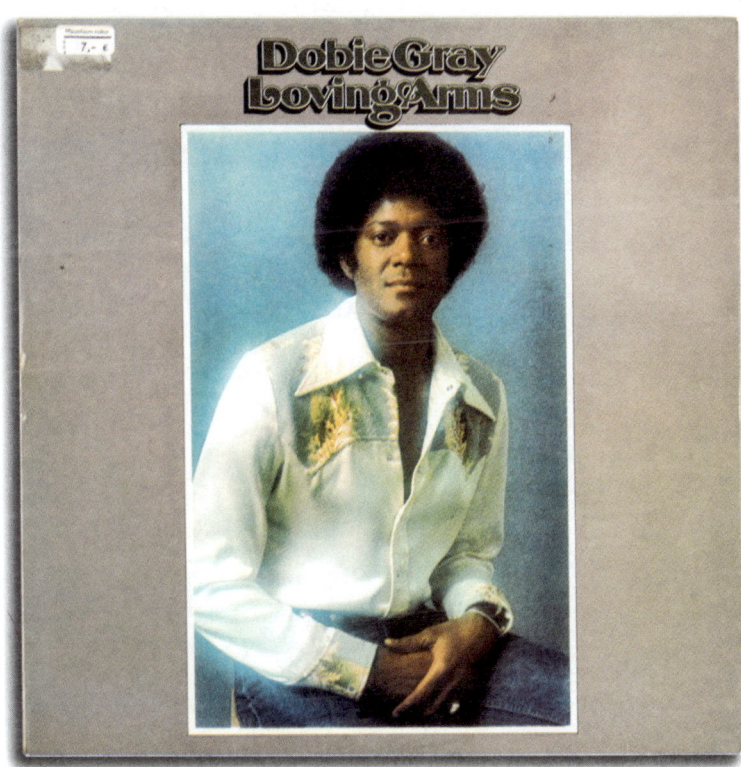

† Dec 6th, 2011
Dobie Gray
Nashville (Tennessee)

Dobie Gray
Loving Arms
MCA Records, 1973
Tom Wilkes (Design)
Rod Dyer, Inc. (Photo)

06   DEC

* Dec 7th, 1988
Benjamin Sainte-Clementine
London (UK)

Benjamin Clementine
I Tell A Fly
Behind Records, 2017
Akatre (Design)
Craig McDean (Photo)

07 DEC

Bill Withers
Justments
Sussex Records, 1974
Carl Overr (Design)
John van Hamersveld (Photo)

08 DEC

Original TV Soundtrack
Diana!
Motown Records, 1971
Harry Langdon (Photo)

09 DEC

OTIS REDDING
THE DOCK OF THE BAY

VOLT 419

† Dec 10th, 1967
Otis Redding
Madison (Wisconsin)

Otis Redding
The Dock Of The Bay
Volt Records, 1968
Loring Euterney (Design)
Jim Marshall (Photo)

10 DEC

* Dec 11th, 1954
Gary (Indiana)

Jermaine Jackson
My Name Is Jermaine
Motown, 1976
Frank Mulvey (Design)
Harry Langdon (Photo)

11 DEC

† Dec 12th, 2007
Ike Turner
San Marcos (California)

Ike & Tina Turner
River Deep Mountain High
A&M Records, 1966
Dennis Hopper (Photo)

12 DEC

Joe Simon
Simon Country
Spring Records, 1973
Cover Artists Unknown

13 DEC

**Jackson 5
Christmas Album**
Tamla Motown, 1970
Cover Artists Unknown

14 DEC

Syl Johnson
We Do It Together
Shama Records, 2017
Cover Artists Unknown

15 DEC

Wendy Rene
After Laughted Comes Tears
Light in The Attic, 2012
Strath Shepard (Design)
Bill Carrier (Photo)

16 DEC

* Dec 17th, 1939
Eddie Kendricks
Montgomery (Alabama)

Eddie Kendricks
People... Hold On
Tamla Motown, 1972
Weldon Arthur McDougal III (Photo)

17 DEC

The Drifters
Up On The Roof
Atlantic Records, 1966
Paragon Publicity (Design)

18 DEC

The Masqueraders
Everybody Wanna Live On
ABC Records, 1975
Martin Donald (Design)
Dave Jarvis (Illustration)

19 DEC

The Quantic Soul Orchestra
Stampede
Thru Thoughts, 2003
Red Design (Design)

20 DEC

* Dec 21st, 1934
Bennie Ross "Hank" Crawford
Memphis (Tennessee)

Hank Crawford
Don't You Worry About A Thing
Kudu, 1974
Rob Ciano (Design)
Pierre Le-Tan (Illustration)

21   DEC

Osibisa
Ojah Awake
Bronze, 1976
Graham Hughes (Design)
Graham Hughes (Photo)

22 DEC

Rocket Juice & The Moon
Honest Jon's Records, 2012
Ogunaja Ademola (Illustration)

23 DEC

∞ STEREO ∞

Merry Christmas the Supremes

- RUDOLPH THE RED-NOSED REINDEER
- CHILDREN'S CHRISTMAS SONG
- THE LITTLE DRUMMER BOY
- BORN OF MARY
- WHITE CHRISTMAS
- SILVER BELLS
- MY FAVORITE THINGS
- TWINKLE TWINKLE LITTLE ME
- JOY TO THE WORLD
- SANTA CLAUS IS COMING TO TOWN
- MY CHRISTMAS TREE
- LITTLE BRIGHT STAR

The Supremes
Merry Christmas
Motown Record Corp., 1965
Cover Artists Unknown

24 DEC

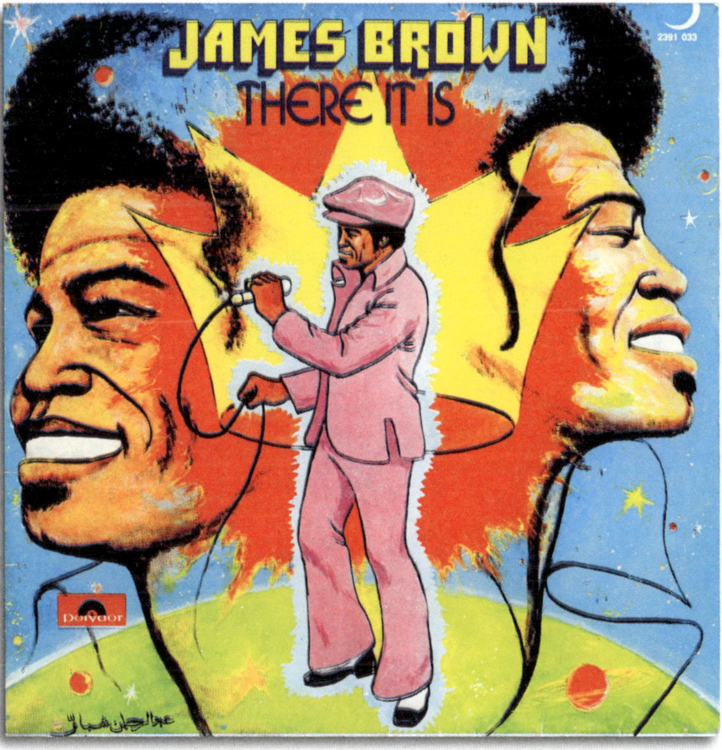

*Dec 25th, 2006
James Joseph Brown Jr.
Atlanta (Georgia)

James Brown
There It Is
Polydor, 1972
Abdul Rahman (Illustration)

25 DEC

Santa's Funk & Soul Christmas Party
The 2nd volume of rare & hip-shaking seasonal grooves

Vol. 2

Various Artists
Santa's Funk & Soul Christmas Party Vol. 2
Tramp Records, 2013
Jan Kohlmeyer (Design)

26 DEC

Sinkane
Mean Love
City Slang, 2014
G. Lofaro (Design)
Shervin Lainez (Photo)

27 DEC

Various Artists
That's Soul 4
Midi, 1973
Froeb & Schmitt (Design)
C.A. Vogel (Photo)

28 DEC

One Way Featuring Al Hudson
MCA Records, 1980
Vartan Kurjian (Illustration)

29 DEC

* Dec 30th, 1928
Ellas Otha Bates
McComb (Mississippi)

Bo Diddley
Where It All Began
Chess, 1972
David Krueger (Design)
Doug Johnson (Illustration)

30 DEC

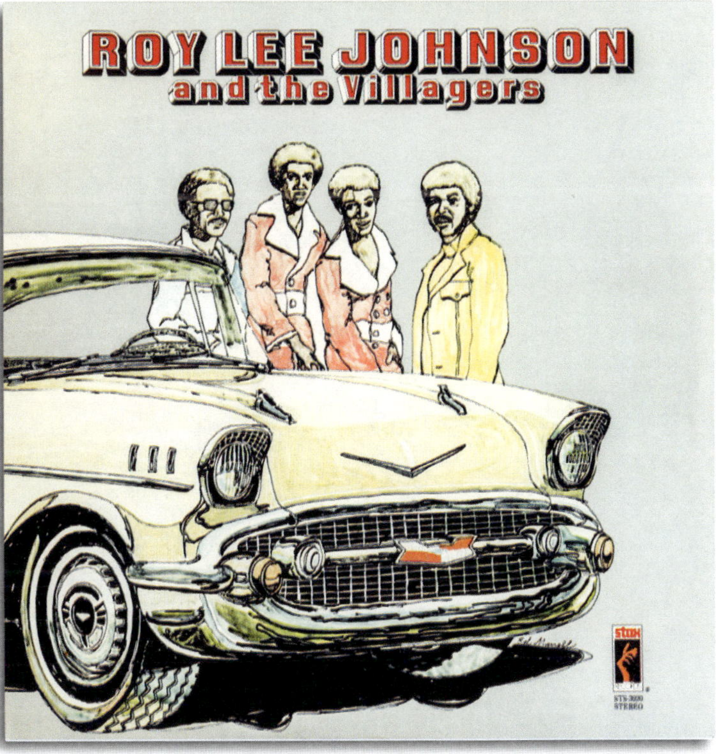

* Dec 31st, 1938
Roy Lee Johnson
Unknown

Roy Lee Johnson and The Villagers
Stax Records, 1973
The Stax Organisation (Design)
Edwin Murrell (Illustration)

31 DEC

Imprint

THE ART OF SOUL COVERS

Seltmann Publishers
Berlin, Germany
www.seltmannpublishers.com
info@seltmannpublishers.com

Cover Artworks & Photographs © by the artists

Cover Photos © by Bernd Jonkmanns
www.berndjonkmanns.com

Cover Selection & Background Research:
Bernd Jonkmanns

Thanks to Johnny Jonkmanns,
Steve Calabretta from Recordstore Back Records (Hamburg),
Ingo Scheel, Paul Rechlin, Christopher Zielske from
Recordstore Plattenrille, HH and Dieter Braun

Art Direction: Sandro Heindel
Print Production by Seltmann Printart

We thank everyone involved for their unique artistic work that made this project possible. If you have any questions or suggestions, please do not hesitate to contact us personally.

This project is an homage to the great and glorious decade of vinyl records and their wonderfully designed covers. With this project, we aim to showcase and preserve the covers as well as their high level of artistic power and profound meaningfulness. Every cover has been selected from personal vinyl collections and individually photographed.

Please note:
Not all bands present themselves on Spotify,
so there are various albums without a code.

© 2024 Seltmann Publishers

ISBN 978-3-949070-54-9

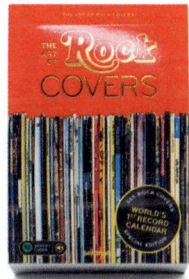

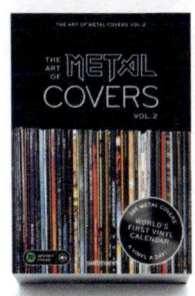

www.seltmannpublishers.com
Worldwide shipping, free within Germany

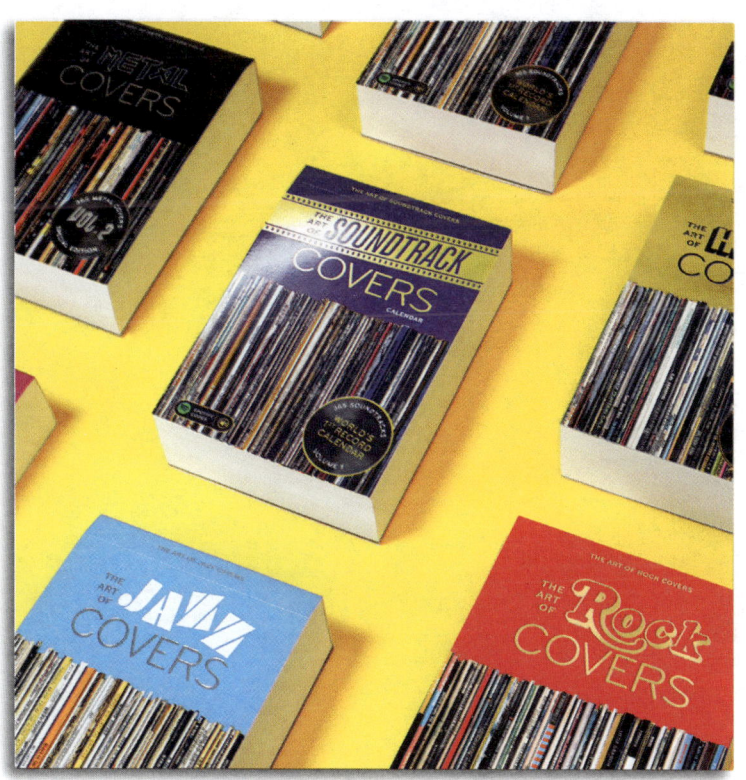

Discover more!

www.seltmannpublishers.com
Worldwide shipping, free within Germany